MW00651432

NOTRE-DAME DE PARIS

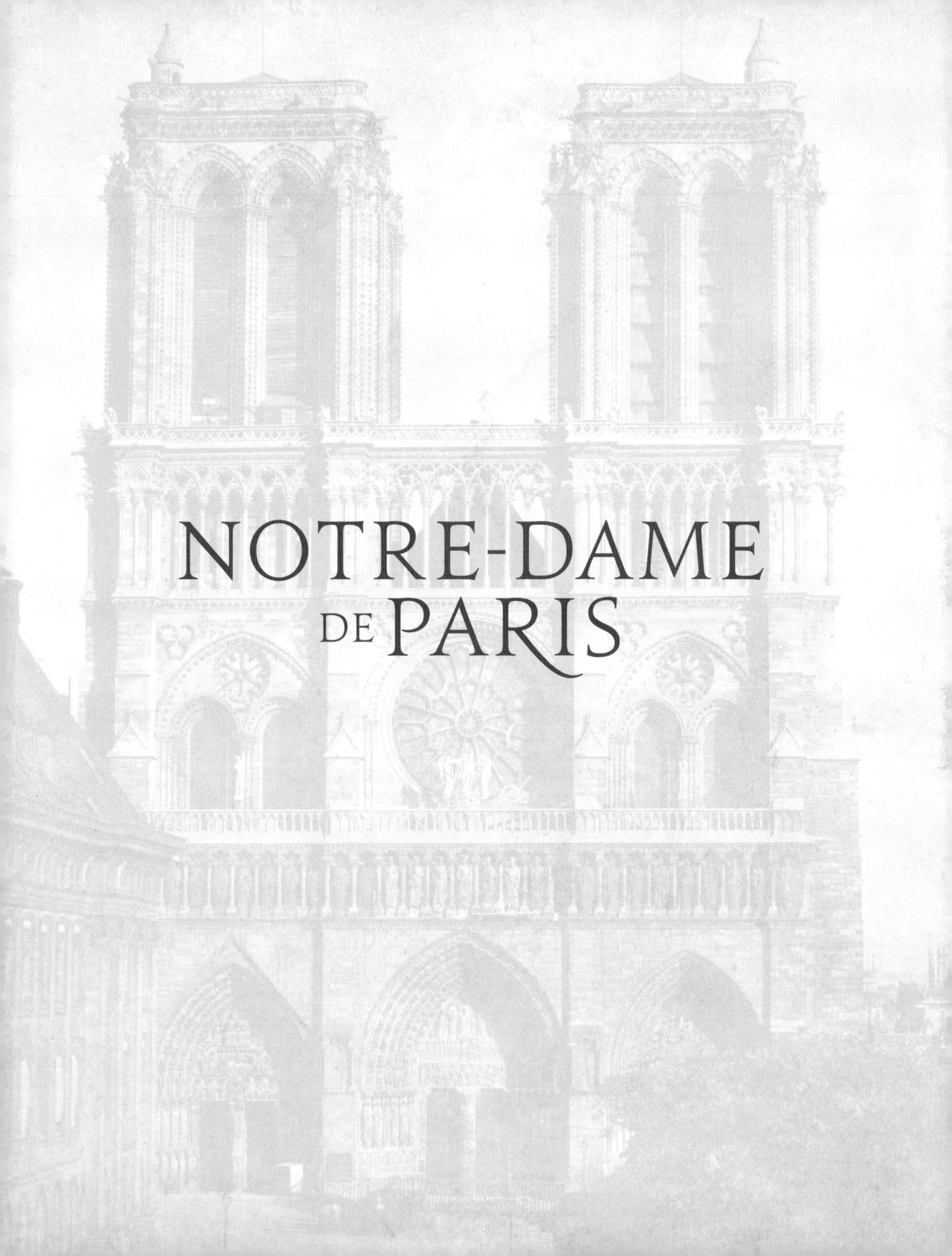

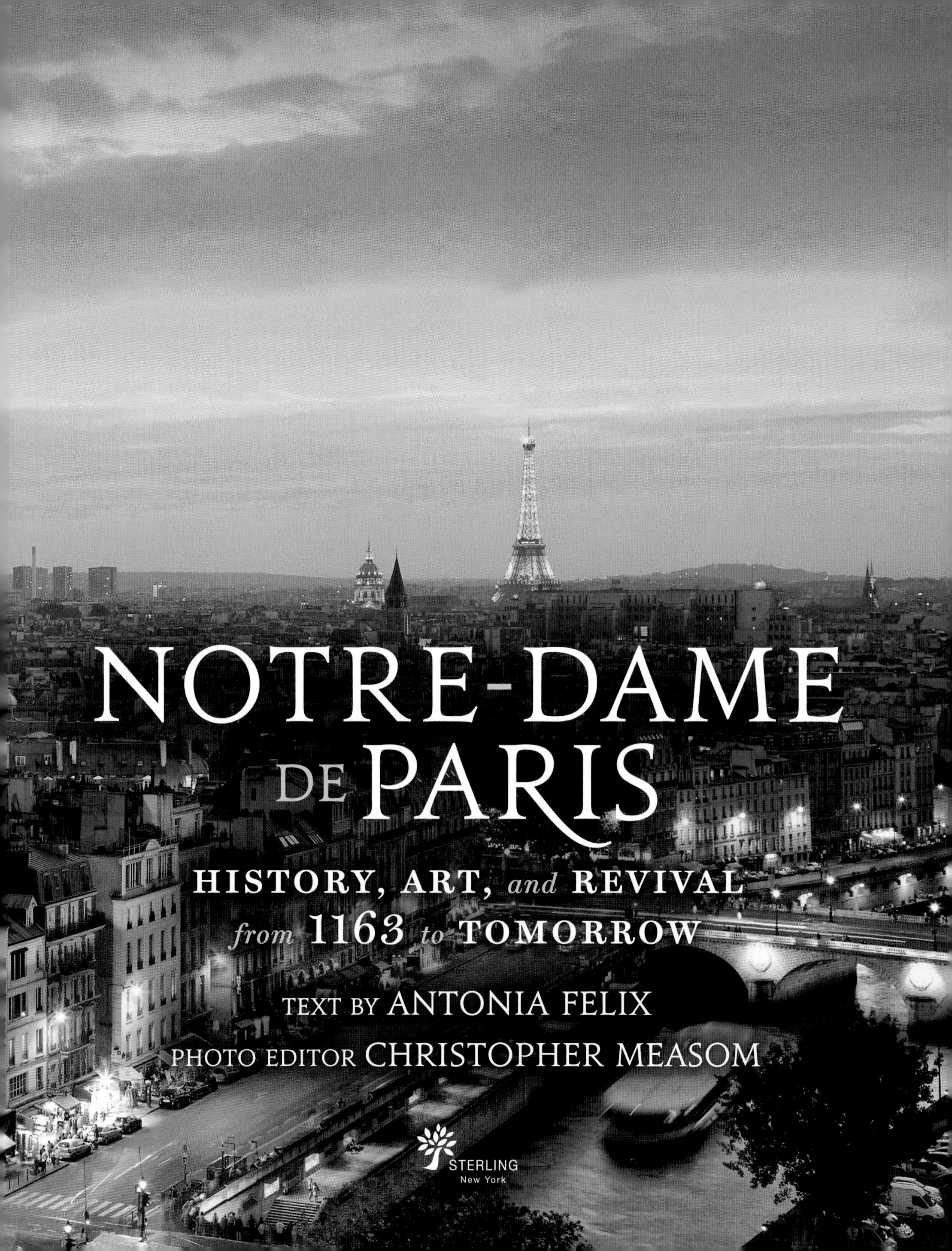

NOTRE-DAME DE PARIS

HISTORY, ART, *and* REVIVAL *from* 1163 *to* TOMORROW

TEXT BY ANTONIA FELIX

PHOTO EDITOR CHRISTOPHER MEASOM

STERLING
New York

STERLING
New York

An Imprint of Sterling Publishing Co., Inc.
1166 Avenue of the Americas
New York, NY 10036

STERLING and the distinctive Sterling logo are registered trademarks of Sterling Publishing Co., Inc.

Text © 2019 Antonia Felix

All rights reserved. No part of this publication may be reproduced, stored in a retrieval system, or transmitted in any form or by any means (including electronic, mechanical, photocopying, recording, or otherwise) without prior written permission from the publisher.

This book is an independent publication and is not associated with or authorized, licensed, sponsored, or endorsed by any person, entity, product, or service mentioned herein. All trademarks are the property of their respective owners, are used for editorial purposes only, and the publisher makes no claim of ownership and shall acquire no right, title, or interest in such trademarks by virtue of this publication.

Excerpt on pages 104–5 from *Brassaï: The Secret Paris of the 30s*, text copyright © 1976 Editions Gallimard, English translation copyright © 1976 Random House Inc., New York and Thames & Hudson Ltd, London. Reprinted by kind permission of Thames & Hudson

Emmanuel Macron speech, pages 156–57 translation © 2019 Antonia Felix and Julie Conrad

ISBN: 978-1-4549-3831-6

Distributed in Canada by Sterling Publishing Co., Inc.
c/o Canadian Manda Group, 664 Annette Street
Toronto, Ontario M6S 2C8, Canada
Distributed in the United Kingdom by GMC Distribution Services
Castle Place, 166 High Street, Lewes, East Sussex BN7 1XU, England
Distributed in Australia by NewSouth Books
University of New South Wales, Sydney, NSW 2052, Australia

For information about custom editions, special sales, and premium and corporate purchases, please contact Sterling Special Sales at 800-805-5489 or specialsales@sterlingpublishing.com.

Manufactured in Canada

2 4 6 8 10 9 7 5 3 1

sterlingpublishing.com

Interior design by Timothy Shaner, NightandDayDesign.biz

Cover design by David Ter-Avanesyan

Picture Credits — see page 175

Contents

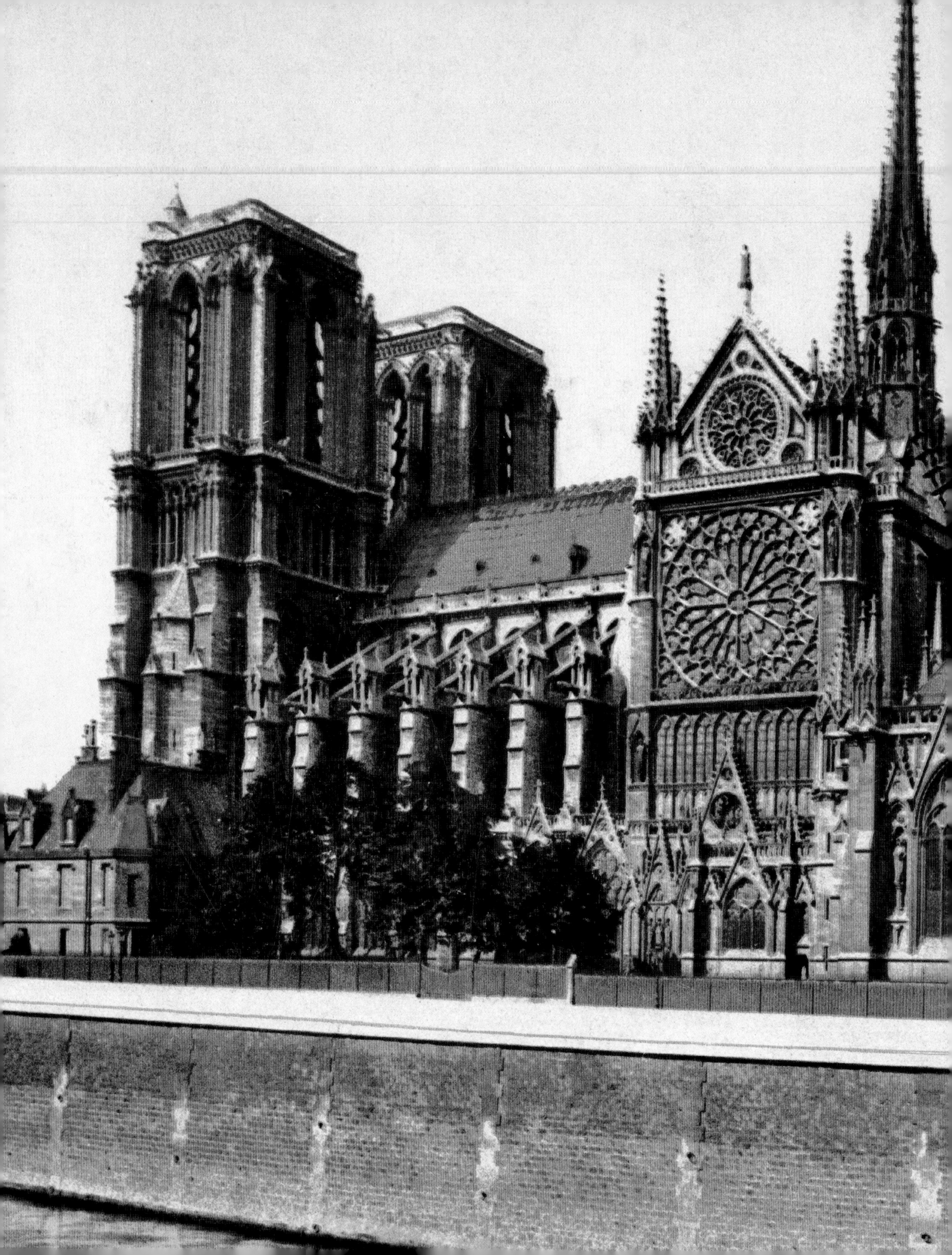

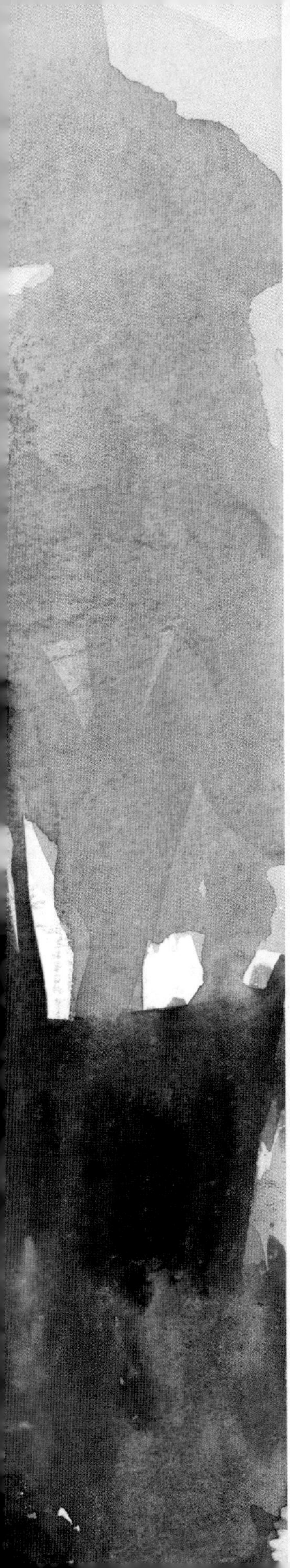

INTRODUCTION

PARADISE ON EARTH

The first time I visited Notre-Dame de Paris, I arrived in the evening for an organ concert. Sitting near the back, I watched people quietly file in, many feeling for the seat with their hands because they could not take their eyes off the ceiling. The first sounds drifted out from the organ loft above and behind us: a slow, flute-like call over a layer of harmony so gentle, so heartrending, that I instinctively turned to the woman sitting next to me. She did the same. Our first response was to share our awe. The cathedral invites these connections, not only with the strangers we see, but also with the invisible ones. As you sit and contemplate the hands that smoothed the pillars, the minds that engineered the soaring vaults, and the pilgrims who stopped to pray there over the centuries, your connection to these past lives is palpable in the colored light.

Each time I return to the cathedral dedicated to Mary at the heart of Paris I feel the same kinship. As so many millions have done, I draw my eyes up, up, and up along the pointed arches that beg us to imagine infinity.

PREVIOUS PAGES: *Photochrom print of Notre-Dame, 1905.* **OPPOSITE:** *Watercolor of the western facade by architect Victor Alfred Lundy, 1949.*

"Gothic architecture . . . aimed at being at the same time colossal and light."

—Jean Bony, art historian

Notre-Dame de Paris is a cathedral among cathedrals, the first to fully integrate the flying buttresses that are a hallmark of Gothic architecture. Pushing against the outer walls like elegant fingers, the flying buttresses allow for thinner, higher walls that can be covered in glass. The rose-shaped windows on three sides of the cathedral were the largest of their time, defying gravity in their intricate lacework moldings. At 226 feet (69 m), the two towers of the western facade, built in the early 1200s, made Notre-Dame the highest building in Paris until the Eiffel Tower was built in 1889.

Like the catlike chimeras perched around its towers, the cathedral has had many lives. Part of Notre-Dame's inspiration comes from its record of triumph and survival, reminding us that while time, neglect, violence, and fire take their toll, they can be healed and mended. In a technological era that brings images of all the needs and horrors of the world literally into our hands, the cathedral stands as a monument to what we can do well and beautifully. At the same time, as one official remarked during the cathedral's 850th anniversary, it is an enduring witness to history, having survived the reigns of "eighty kings, two emperors, and five republics."

The most famous ceremony in the cathedral's history, the self-coronation of Napoleon Bonaparte as emperor in 1804, lives on in a work of art Bonaparte commissioned at the time. Jacques-Louis David's large painting of the coronation (see pages 52–53), which details the opulent interior of the cathedral as staged for the event, now hangs in the Louvre in Paris.

While Notre-Dame embodies centuries of political, cultural, and religious history—and remains a living church where Mass is celebrated every day—the nature of the building itself has an equally strong impact. The master builders designed the cathedral with geometry based on certain forms in nature: forms, the builders believed, that constituted the foundational language of the universe. This sacred geometry, the language of God, created harmonies that we can visibly see

and also unconsciously sense. The cathedral was meant to be a paradise on earth. Its earthly squares and heavenly circles are saturated with the medieval love for Mary.

After the devastating fire of April 2019, people across the world are watching to see what the future may hold for Notre-Dame de Paris, which has found another surge of popularity equal to that inspired by Victor Hugo's 1831 novel *Notre-Dame de Paris*, translated into English as *The Hunchback of Notre-Dame*. Like Hugo's protagonist Quasimodo, we have come to know the cathedral in intimate detail. We are the latest generation to imbue it "with a familiar spirit" in yet another new century.

ABOVE: *One of the earliest known photographic images of Notre-Dame de Paris, c. 1838, by Louis Daguerre.*

MEDIEVAL MASTERPIECE

LA VILLE · CITE · VNIVERSITE · DE PARIS
LA BASTILLE
LES TOVRNELLES
LE LOVVRE
LA TOVR DV BOIS
LES TVILLERIES
LA TOVR NELLE
LE PREAV CLERS
OCCIDENS
Le sainct senat ou sont les Conseilliers
Nombre six vingts hommes tresinguliers,
De grand sçauoir, qui tiennent leur office
De par le Roy, pour faire à tous iustice
Sur les proces à la court intimez
Aultres gens sont en iustice estimez
Tenant le lieu du grant preuost royal
Pour ordonner leur iugement loyal
A toutes gens selon leur cause bonne
Apres ya mainte docte personne
Estudiant aux loix pour ce establir
Et de sçauoir sont tresfort ennoblir.
Dedens Paris les sciences florissent
Et gens sçauans en ce lieu resplandissent
Plus qu'en nul lieu, car Palas y octroye
Autant ou plus qu'en Athenes ou Troye
Le sien seiour: & les muses sçauantes
Font en ce lieu leur demeure tenantes,
Plus que iamais ne furent sur le mond
De Aonias, ou par elle semond
Estoit iadis maint homme pour apprendre,
Arts & mestiers, apres nous fault comprendre,
Desquelz il vient tresgrande vtilité
Au lieu susdict aussy tranquilité,
Semblablement marchans de toutes guises
Viennent illec pour toutes marchandises
Distribuer, & tant de peuple abonde
En cestuy lieu qu'il n'ya peuple au monde
Qui soit autant à chascun gratieuse
Qu'est ceste cy, ny autant spatieuse.
Icy est le vray pourtraict naturel de la ville, cité, vniuersité
& Faubourgz de Paris, ou sont iustement figurées toutes les Rues & Ruelles correspondãtes
l'vne à l'autre, ainsi qui sont de present situées, qui sont en nõbre deux cens quatre vingtz &
sept. Pareillement sont figurées toutes les Eglises, & Monasteres, qui sont en nombre cent
quatre. Aussy sont figurez tous les Colleges, qui sont en nõbre quarante neuf. Et pour con-
gnoistre icelles Rues, Ruelles, Eglises, Monasteres & Colleges, vous trouuerrez leurs noms
escriptz à chũn sur son propre endroict. Cõme plus amplement vous pouez voir cy dessus.
A Paris, par Oliuier Truschet, & Germain Hoyau, demourans en
la Rue de Montorgueil, au Chef sainct Denys.

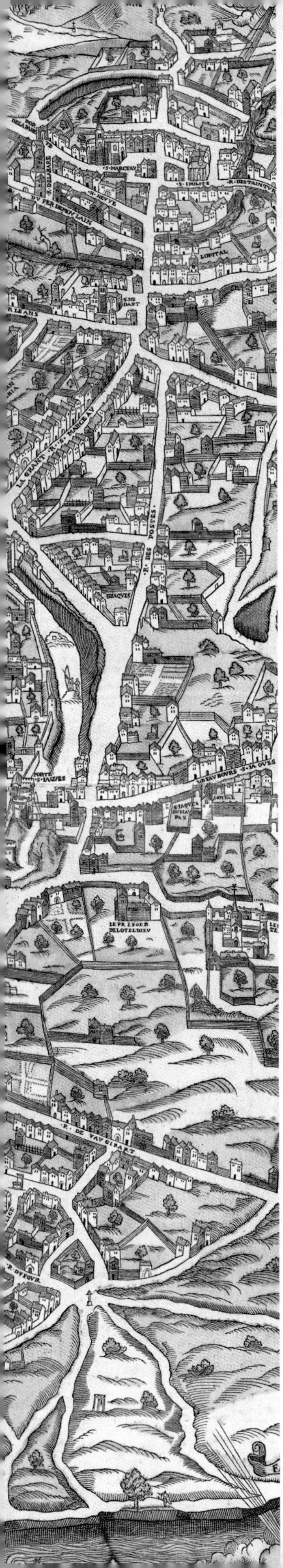

FOUNDATIONS

Notre-Dame stands on the east end of the tiny Île de la Cité (Island of the City) in the center of the Seine, which divides Paris into two halves: the Rive Gauche and Rive Droite, or Left Bank and Right Bank. The island, just three-fourths of a mile (1.2 km) long and shaped like a ship with its pointed bow headed west, has been home to sacred sites since the Parisii, a tribe of Gallic Celts, settled there some time around 250 BCE, bringing with them their Celtic gods and goddesses. By the time the Romans conquered Gaul in 50 BCE, the Parisii had developed the island town the Romans called Lutetia (possibly Celtic for "houses midstream") into a busy port center that minted its own gold coins.

After conquering Lutetia, the Romans chose the small hill on the island's eastern edge to build a temple to Jupiter, although worship of the Celtic gods and goddesses remained, according to a first-century artifact found during excavations below Notre-Dame in 1710. The dig exposed pieces of a structure dedicated to Jupiter and Tiberius, the Roman emperor who ruled from 14 to 37 CE. Erected by the

PREVIOUS PAGES: L'Abside *[Apse]* de Notre-Dame de Paris, *1854, one of a series of etchings of Paris that Charles Méryon created after being inspired by Victor Hugo.* **OPPOSITE:** *This map of Paris, created by Olivier Truschet and Germain Hoyau around the year 1550, shows the Île de la Cité at the center and Notre-Dame at the top right portion of the island.*

guild of Lutetian sailor-merchants, the Pilier des Nautes (Pillar of the Boatmen), which once stood seventeen feet (5 m) tall, was covered in images of both Roman and Celtic deities. Carvings of the Roman gods Mercury and Vulcan are depicted alongside Gaul warriors, druids in their crowns and garb, and the horned Celtic god Cernunnos. The pieces, which may have been part of an altar, are on view at the Musée de Cluny in Paris. Other discoveries of Celtic religious art found throughout Western Europe show us the dedication to several types of pre-Christian mother

ABOVE: *Pencil drawing of ancient bas-relief sculptures found under Notre-Dame Cathedral in 1710. The sculptures, dating from the first century, were originally part of a column known as the Pilier des Nautes that was given as tribute from the local Parisii tribe's mariners guild (Nautes de Lutèce) to Tiberius, the Roman emperor. A mix of Celtic (Esus, Cernunnos, Tarvos) and Roman (Lovis or Jupiter, Volcanus or Valcanus) deities are depicted on the column.* **OPPOSITE:** *Detail of a lithograph from 1861 by Félix Benoist showing the Basilica Saint-Denis.*

goddesses either sitting or standing with a child in their arms. The images have endured across time and faiths; a relief sculpture of the Virgin Mary sitting on a throne and holding the Christ child on the Portal of Saint Anne has greeted visitors to the cathedral since the early thirteenth century.

The first Christian church on the Île de la Cité was built on the Roman temple site, possibly in the fourth century, and dedicated to the first Christian martyr Saint Stephen (Étienne in French). Massive for its time, the Cathedral of Saint Stephen took up approximately half the floor space of the present Notre-Dame Cathedral and contained jet-black columns that reflected the chips of color set in the small windows, ornate mosaic floors, and a roof made of gilt-coated French oak timber. In the seventh century, the Parisians built two smaller churches next to Saint Stephen, one of which, Notre-Dame, is considered the first church in Paris dedicated to Mary. This first Notre-Dame didn't survive a Viking raid of the city in 856, when

the French negotiated their terms of surrender. The Parisians could keep only three of their churches, and the island's Notre-Dame was not among them. Even as the Vikings continued to attack Paris in the ninth century, the city rebuilt Notre-Dame from the ashes and transferred the seat of the Paris bishop from Saint Stephen's to the rebuilt church in 868 CE. The popularity of Mary's church was on the rise.

The city continued to expand outward from the Île de la Cité across both banks, and in 1160, the new bishop of Paris became committed to building a new cathedral. Bishop Maurice de Sully (d. 1196) was inspired by the newly reconstructed abbey at Saint-Denis, just north of Paris—the structure that is widely considered the prototype of French Gothic. The church at the Saint-Denis monastery was the most prestigious in medieval France: it was closely aligned with the monarchy; held the relics of Saint Denis, one of the patron saints of France; and was the burial place of kings and queens. Abbot Suger (c. 1081–1151), who directed the construction of the Saint-Denis basilica, needed to enlarge the space to accommodate the massive crowds that poured in during feast days to see the holy relics; he also envisioned the new church as a reflection of spiritual and political power. At the same time, Suger sought to create a building that expressed the theology of light, the idea that the contemplation of light is a way of understanding God.

The result at Saint-Denis was a design that opened up the space inside the church, both horizontally and vertically, and allowed large stained glass windows to light the interior. The pointed arches, ribbed vaults, and sculpted facade of Saint-Denis existed in other churches in France, but they had never before been brought together as a unified design. Within decades, the style had spread to Chartres, Noyon, Senlis, Laon, Paris, and then to every country in Europe.

In addition to the theological idea about light as a pathway to God, the radical innovations of Gothic style in the cathedrals were also shaped, in part, by the era's fervent devotion to the Virgin Mary. American historian Henry Adams (1838–1918) described this passionate zeal for Mary as the people's response to a religion founded on a strict, judgmental Holy Trinity:

OPPOSITE: The Right Hand of God Protecting the Faithful against the Demons *by Jean Fouquet, from the illuminated manuscript* Hours of Étienne Chevalier, *c. 1452–60. The hand of God can be seen above as the faithful pray and demons flee against the backdrop of medieval Paris, including Notre-Dame.*

Their attachment to Mary rested on an instinct of self-preservation. They knew their own peril. If there was to be a future life, Mary was their only hope. She alone represented Love. The Trinity were, or was, One, and could, by the nature of its essence, administer justice alone. Only childlike illusion could expect a personal favour from Christ. . . . Call the three Godheads by what names one liked, still they must remain One; must administer one justice; must admit only one law. In that law, no human weakness or error could exist; by its essence it was infinite, eternal, immutable. There was no crack and no cranny in the system, through which human frailty could hope for escape. One was forced from corner to corner by a remorseless logic until one fell helpless at Mary's feet.

In Paris, Bishop Sully initiated and managed the project of building a new cathedral dedicated to Mary in the magnificent new style of the abbey at Saint-Denis and a handful of cathedrals in northern France. Elected as bishop in 1160, Sully had risen from humble beginnings to attend school with the future king Louis VII and become his lifelong friend. He earned a reputation in Paris as a brilliant professor of theology and one of the most popular preachers of his time. His sermons were copied and sent throughout France and England. With the help of King Louis VII, the prosperous community of Paris, income from the cathedral's properties, gifts from wealthy supporters outside Paris, and a widespread mission program for collecting donations, Sully was able to raise enough money to start building the cathedral in 1163.

During those three years of fundraising and planning, Sully held meetings with church officials (and possibly the king) to decide the scale of the new Notre-Dame.

They agreed to build a larger cathedral than Saint-Denis, a building so large that constructing and fitting it would require tearing down part of the seven-foot- (2 m) high Roman wall surrounding the island and building a new road for transporting materials. "There is

no more striking symbol of the twelfth century's willingness to dispense with the confining past than the breaching of this ancient wall," wrote architectural critic Allan Temko in *Notre-Dame of Paris* (1955).

Bishop Sully did not live to see the cathedral completed before his death in 1196—far from it. Nearly 150 years of building would continue before the work was finished, but his mark may have been left for history to see on the western facade, set in stone on the portal of Saint Anne. Glancing up, the figure to the left of Mary holding a bishop's staff is believed by some to be Sully, and the kneeling figure at the right may be King Louis VII.

OPPOSITE: Vierge de Notre-Dame de Paris, *a nineteenth-century drawing of the sculpture of the Virgin Mary (Notre Dame) by architect and interior designer Charles Percier.* **ABOVE:** *The tympanum of the Saint-Anne Portal, the doorway on the right side of the western facade, created around 1150 for Saint Stephen's Cathedral but repurposed in 1200 for Notre-Dame. It depicts the Virgin and Child at center with angels at their side, and to the left possibly Bishop Sully. The lintels below depict the marriages of Anne and Joachim (Mary's parents) and Mary and Joseph.*

C C

What Lies Below

The Cathedral Crypt

What started as a dig for an underground parking lot in 1965 turned out to be one of the most dramatic discoveries in Paris history. Workers excavating beneath the front square of Notre-Dame de Paris uncovered ruins that archeologists identified as remnants of the city's history dating back two thousand years. The Archeological Crypt, opened to the public in 1980, spans the length of a football field and reveals how Paris developed through the centuries.

The oldest section of the crypt contains a stone remnant of a port built in 42 BCE, followed by remnants of ancient Roman streets from the first century that offer a glimpse of the city called Lutetia. Sections of Roman baths from the fourth century, including the underground heating system, are exposed in detail, and the remains of a wall built to fortify the Île de la Cité in the third century show how the island defended itself from Germanic invasions. The foundations of homes and buildings torn down in the twelfth century to make room for the new cathedral expose layers of medieval life, just as the basements of buildings removed during cathedral renovations at the time of Napoleon III reveal details of structures that disappeared in the nineteenth century.

Visitors who appreciate the historical aspects of Notre-Dame de Paris will find the deepest roots of that history in the Archeological Crypt.

> "The human race has never conceived an important thought that it has not written down in stone."
>
> —Victor Hugo, *Notre-Dame de Paris* (*The Hunchback of Notre Dame*), 1831

OPPOSITE: *The Gallo-Roman ruins of Notre-Dame's crypt.*

"I wish to honor these stones, so lovingly transformed into masterpieces by humble and wise artisans . . . these beautiful lingering shadows where softness sleeps at the heart of power."

—Auguste Rodin, *Cathedrals of France*, 1914 (1965)

ÉCOLE NATIONALE DES BEAUX-ARTS
33968
BIBLIOTHÈQUE
5058

Paris. 1908

Eglise Notre Dame. (11me Arrt)

PREVIOUS PAGES: *Photo of Notre-Dame at night from the Pont de l'Archevêché by Marcel Fleureau, c. 1935.* **OPPOSITE:** *A photograph inside Notre-Dame titled* Notre Dame Voeu de Louis XIII *by Eugène Atget, 1908.* **ABOVE:** *Photochrom of the interior of Notre-Dame, c. 1890–1900.*

Author Victor Hugo on Gothic Architecture

Excerpt from *Notre-Dame de Paris* [known as *The Hunchback of Notre-Dame*], 1831

In these pages from his blockbuster novel, Victor Hugo (1802–85) offered a history lesson on architecture as a reflection of the times. The Romanesque style of the early Middle Ages that imitated the solid, heavy rounded forms of Roman architecture gave way to French Gothic and a new focus on light, soaring lines, and artistry. The Gothic style reflected the spirit of innovation that arose during the Crusades—a period that brought an influx of new ideas.

During [the Middle Ages'] first period, while theocracy is organizing Europe, while the Vatican is collecting and gathering round it the elements of a new Rome, constructed out of the Rome which lay in fragments round the Capitol, while Christianity goes forth to search among the ruins of a former civilization, and out of its remains to build up a new hierarchic world of which sacerdotalism is the keystone, we hear it stirring faintly through the chaos; then gradually, from under the breath of Christianity, from under the hands of the barbarians, out of the rubble of dead architectures, Greek and Roman—there emerges that mysterious Romanesque architecture, sister of the theocratic buildings of Egypt and India, inalterable emblem of pure Catholicism, immutable hieroglyph of papal unity. The whole tendency of the time is written in this sombre Romanesque style. Everywhere it represents authority, unity, the imperturbable, the absolute, Gregory VII; always the priest, never the man: everywhere the caste, never the people.

Then come the Crusades, a great popular movement, and every popular movement, whatever its cause or its aim, has as its final precipitation the spirit of liberty.

OPPOSITE: Notre-Dame de Paris, *an 1881 drawing by Luc-Olivier Merson inspired by this passage from Victor Hugo's novel: "The transept belfry and the two towers were to him three great cages, the birds in which, taught by him, would sing for him alone."*

Innovations struggled forth to the light. . . . Authority totters, unity is split and branches off into two directions. Feudalism demands to divide the power with theocracy before the inevitable advent of the people, who, as ever, will take the lion's share. . . . Hence we see feudalism thrusting up through theocracy, and the people's power again through feudalism. The whole face of Europe is altered. Very good; the face of architecture alters with it. Like civilization, she has turned a page, and the new spirit of the times finds her prepared to write to his dictation. She has brought home with her from the crusades the pointed arch, as the nations have brought free thought. Henceforward, as Rome is gradually dismembered, so the Romanesque architecture dies out. . . . The Cathedral itself, once so imbued with dogma, invaded now by the commonalty, by the spirit of freedom, escapes from the priest, and falls under the dominion of the artist. The artist fashions it after his own good pleasure. Farewell to mystery, to myth, to rule. . . . Provided the priest has his basilica and his altar, he has nothing further to say in the matter. The four walls belong to the artist. The stone book belongs no more to the priest, to religion, to Rome, but to imagination, to poetry, to the people. From thenceforward occur these rapid and innumerable transformations of an architecture only lasting three centuries, so striking after the six or seven centuries of stagnant immobility of the Romanesque style. Meanwhile, Art marches on with giant strides, and popular originality plays what was formerly the Bishop's part. . . .

"In those days, he who was born a poet became an architect."

This was the only form . . . in which free thought was possible, and therefore found full expression only in those books called edifices. . . . Therefore, having but this one outlet, it rushed towards it from all parts; and hence the countless mass of Cathedrals spread over all Europe, a number so prodigious that it seems incredible, even after verifying it with one's own eyes. All the material, all the intellectual forces of society, converged to that one point—architecture. In this way, under the pretext of building churches to the glory of God, the art developed to magnificent proportions.

In those days, he who was born a poet became an architect.

Anonymous print titled View of Notre-Dame de Paris, *1675–1711.*

Hand-colored lithograph by Charles Rivière showing the south side of Notre-Dame with pedestrians on the street in the foreground, c. 1870s.

MASTER BUILDERS

One of the earliest daring achievements of the French Gothic style, Notre-Dame was designed by master builders who led the work with their teams of expert craftsmen. New ideas and techniques brought to France during the Crusades expanded the master builders' vision of what was possible—colossal size, especially in terms of height. These masters were trained in design methods that used regular shapes—particularly the square—as the single "module" from which all the proportions of a building were drafted. "The knowledge of this way of determining proportions," wrote twentieth-century German art historian Otto von Simson, "was considered so essential that it was kept a professional secret." The masters used the term "according to true measure" to describe using one square as the basis of all the proportions in the design. The work of the Notre-Dame master builders also included selecting stone from quarries as near as the Left Bank and as far as Arcueil, five miles (8 km) south. The stonecutters dressed each stone with exquisite accuracy where it stood; afterward, it was hoisted onto an oxcart and pulled into the city, ready to be placed.

Master builders also knew how to cut stone and, in addition to understanding the geometry for design, were trained in the technical skills of laying foundations and designing supports and scaffolding.

The front entrance of Notre-Dame, 2017.

While renowned master builders were commissioned for cathedrals throughout Europe, held a higher place in society than their craftsmen, and became famous for their work, there is no record of the names of the four masters who worked on Notre-Dame for the first eighty-seven years. After 1250 and through the cathedral's completion in 1345, however, the master builders were known to be Jean de Chelles, Pierre de Montreuil, Pierre de Chelles, Jean Ravy, and Jean le Bouteiller.

Like all medieval churches, Notre-Dame de Paris is a visual encyclopedia of Christianity, designed by visionary builders to communicate through symbol and story. The cathedral lies on an east-west axis, with the semicircular recess called the apse at the eastern end of the structure. The altar, at the front of the apse, is set eastward to direct everyone's attention toward the rising sun, a symbol of life and of Christ as the light of the world. The western end of the cathedral, facing the setting sun, symbolizes death, hence the positioning of the Last Judgment as the sculptural theme on the western facade's central portal. Cutting across the main axis, the north-south transept gives the cathedral the shape of a Latin cross, although the original transept at Notre-Dame only barely jutted out at the sides. This rectangular piece divides the interior into two main sections, the choir and the nave.

The first language of the cathedral is its geometry, since the master builders of the Middle Ages based their designs (both for length and height) on squares, equilateral triangles, and circles. Because these shapes reflected the divine proportions of the human being and the patterns of nature, their geometric principles and mathematical ratios were thought to be, as architect and architectural historian Nelly Shafik Ramzy writes, "the dominant ratios of the universe." The master builders used this sacred geometry to make the perfection of God visible on earth and, in the process, allow parishioners to experience this divine force embedded in the cathedral.

ABOVE: God as Architect/Builder/Geometer/Craftsman, *the frontispiece of the Bible moralisée, representing God as creator of the world, c. 1220–30.* **OPPOSITE:** *View from above Notre-Dame highlighting the Roman cross shape of the cathedral, 2017.*

Notre-Dame de Paris

Notre-Dame was built in the same shape as the older Romanesque cathedrals, but was designed to be far taller and lighter, with pointed arches and vaults, and stained glass windows to let in more light.

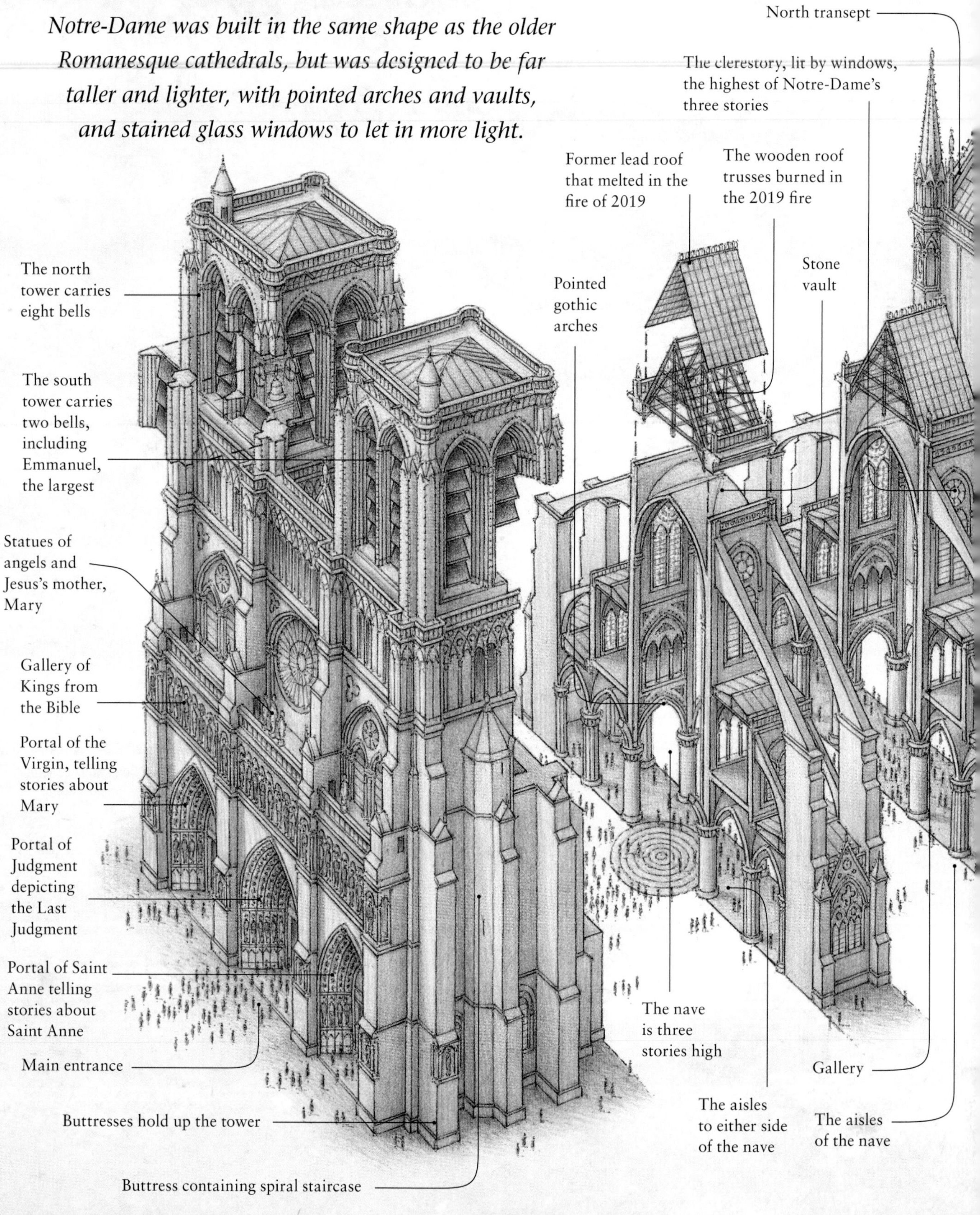

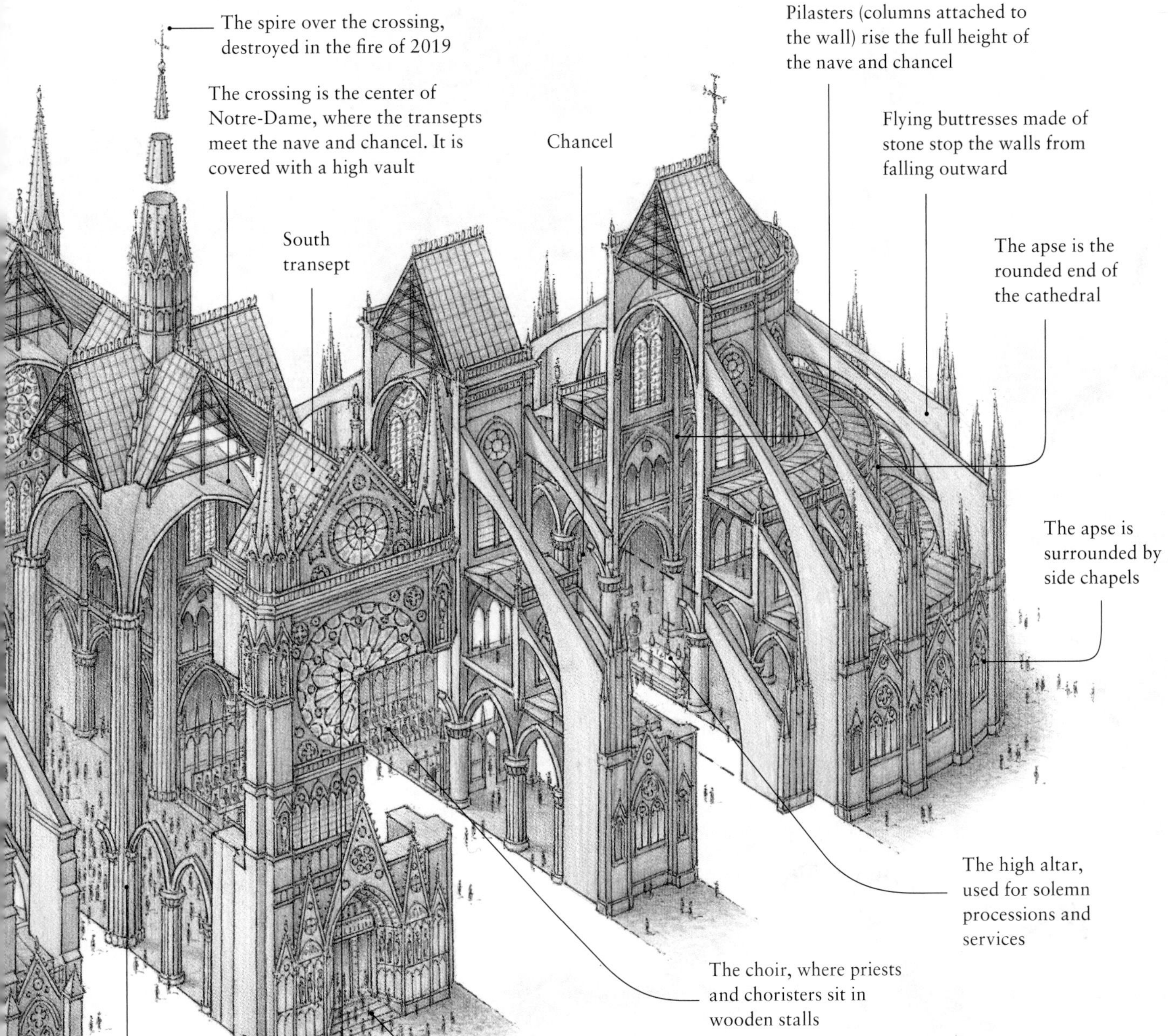
The spire over the crossing, destroyed in the fire of 2019
The crossing is the center of Notre-Dame, where the transepts meet the nave and chancel. It is covered with a high vault
South transept
Chancel
Pilasters (columns attached to the wall) rise the full height of the nave and chancel
Flying buttresses made of stone stop the walls from falling outward
The apse is the rounded end of the cathedral
The apse is surrounded by side chapels
The high altar, used for solemn processions and services
The choir, where priests and choristers sit in wooden stalls
Portal of Saint Stephen
The main arcade is supported on columns
South Rose window filled with stained glass

Complete Building

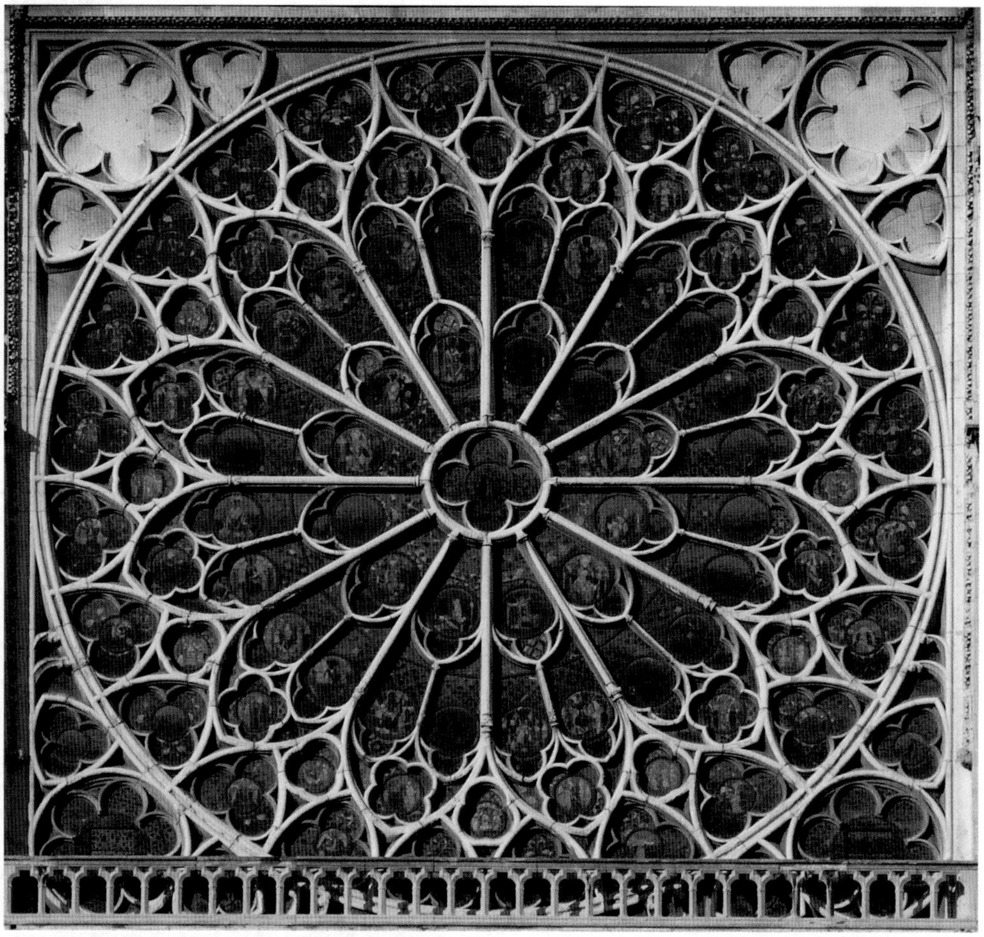

The Gothic cathedral was many things at once: a model of the celestial city, God's home on Earth; a ship carrying the community of believers through their spiritual journey and the storms of life; a safe place for holy relics and other treasures of the Church; and a biblical storybook of images for the illiterate population. "If the Gothic architect designed his sanctuary according to the laws of harmonious proportion, he did not only imitate the perfection of the visible world but also created an image . . . of an invisible one," wrote Otto von Simson.

The same ideas of divine ratios applied to the music composed in the Middle Ages, with the satisfying sense of the octave, perfect fourth, and perfect fifth a reflection of the divine perfection of those intervals, or ratios. (In fact, the philosophy of divine musical intervals came first, inspiring the study of physical proportions that became sacred geometry.) Divine musical and architectural harmony went hand in hand in the music and structure of the cathedrals.

The sacred geometry of Notre-Dame may not be instantly recognizable, but one clear example is found at the entrance with its central rose window. A true square can only be made by first drawing a circle, and this relationship between the two is immediately seen on the window of the western facade. The square represents the created world and its limited nature, and the circle represents the unlimited, perfect nature of God. The cathedral combines both meanings by setting the round rose window within a square. The total effect symbolizes the story of Mary's role in Christianity: God (circle) joined the created world (square) by becoming man. Mary, who appears seated with Jesus in the center of the window (right), said yes to God in bringing Jesus into the world. In her window facing the city, she introduces Jesus to the world.

The floor plan drawn up by the first master builder overlapped slightly with the roofless, decaying Cathedral of Saint Stephen, which was preserved long enough to be used as a bustling workshop when building began. The smaller, original Notre-Dame was torn down and its stones recycled for the new project. Before building could begin, workers dug a foundation thirty feet (9 m) deep and filled it with carefully cut stones for a footing powerful enough to hold a tall cathedral. The massive workforce that crowded onto the island included plasterers, masons,

OPPOSITE: *Exterior view of the Rose Sud or Rose du Midi, the south rose window, a gift of King Louis IX. It was completely rebuilt in 1861 by Viollet-le-Duc, and little of the original glass remains.* **ABOVE:** *Detail of the western rose window, the first built and smallest of the cathedral's three rose windows. It was originally completed around 1220 and reconstructed between 1844 and 1867.*

> "A medieval church was not intended to be gray and formal, but a riot of color."
>
> —Alice Mary Hilton, Art Historian

mortar makers, glassmakers, painters, and laborers who did basic jobs like transporting and digging.

The foundation stone was laid in 1163 in a ceremony led by Sully and his nephew, with Pope Alexander III perhaps in attendance, and the building was constructed from east to west. The semicircular apse that shapes the east side of the cathedral, and the choir, came first. Eleven years later, this section was completed and Bishop Sully assisted in consecrating the altar that stood in the apse. Columns were placed to shape two curving aisles called ambulatories, the walking passages behind and on either side of the altar. The next phase created a large section of the nave, the main section of the cathedral, along with its five aisles—one in the center and two on each outer side. The third and fourth phases completed the nave, the western facade, the two towers and spire, and the highest windows. From 1250 to 1345, work included building a set of chapels in the choir and, on the outside of that section, buttresses to support its walls.

The cathedral ceiling is a network of masonry ribs that rise up from slender pillars in a fluid upward movement. Outside, flying buttresses take up the thrust from the weight of the ceiling, a Gothic element that allowed for thinner walls covered in windows and greater height. Above it all, the steep and enormously heavy lead roof was supported by the "Forest," a frame of beams cut from three- to four-hundred-year-old oak trees in the region's ancient forests.

Four levels high with a space that seemed to sweep to heaven, gleaming outside with its brightly painted statuary and towers, and coloring the atmosphere inside and out with its breathtaking rose windows, the finished cathedral towered over the city as a unified work of art.

OPPOSITE: *A new LED lighting system installed in 2014 brings more light to the cathedral, and the basic white light can be adjusted to a dynamic range of color for special events.*

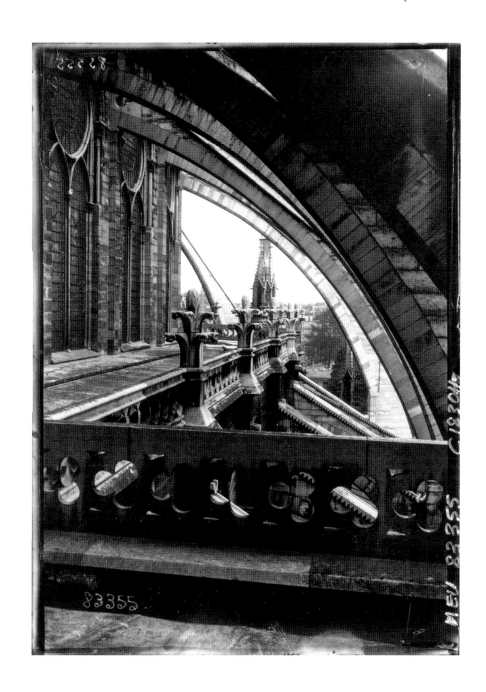

OPPOSITE: *Photograph by Édouard Baldus in the 1860s.* ABOVE: *A view of the cathedral's flying buttresses commissioned by the press agency Agence Meurisse, 1920.* FOLLOWING PAGES: *The vaulted ceiling and stained glass inside Notre-Dame, 2013.*

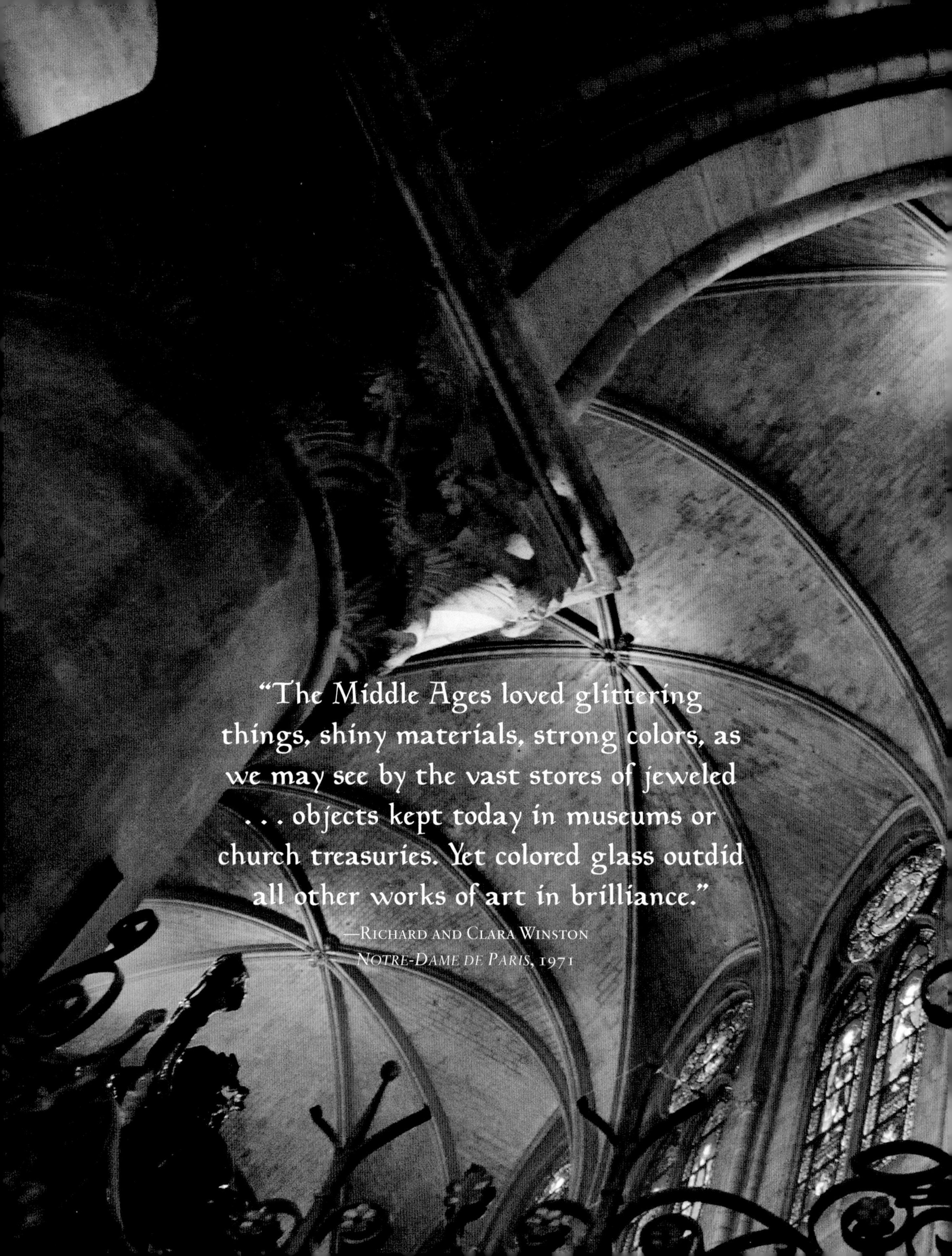

"The Middle Ages loved glittering things, shiny materials, strong colors, as we may see by the vast stores of jeweled . . . objects kept today in museums or church treasuries. Yet colored glass outdid all other works of art in brilliance."

—Richard and Clara Winston
Notre-Dame de Paris, 1971

Stained Glass

When master builder Jean de Chelles began a new phase of construction at Notre-Dame de Paris in c. 1250, the structure as planned by Maurice de Sully had largely been built. But the cathedral was not complete in the eyes of a master builder eager to integrate the advancements in architecture that had developed over the previous ninety years. The masters had solved all the structural problems and were now focused on refinement, especially in terms of replacing stone walls and their minimal windows with walls made almost completely of stained glass.

The master builder who had designed the first of Notre-Dame's three rose windows, the west rose above the portals of the western facade, may have been Jean's uncle, according to Allan Temko. Whoever built the west rose, which was completed in c. 1220, used a radically new design that for the first time opened up a tremendous amount of wall space, more than thirty feet (9 m), to house a window in a strong but delicate frame. The glass artists designing the west rose set the virgin and child at the center, surrounding her with twelve prophets and additional rings depicting the seasons, virtues and vices, and signs of the zodiac.

Inspired by the new capabilities for large glasswork, Jean de Chelles planned a bold design for the north and west walls of the transept. "The offer of more light was irresistible," wrote Temko. "All over France at this time, monuments . . . were being rebuilt, simply for the sake of more illumination." In 1250, Chelles propped up the vaults with timbers, tore down the northern and southern facades, and installed the largest open rose windows ever built. Both windows measure forty-three feet (13 m) in diameter and, like the west rose, are predominantly blue glsss with reds, greens, browns, purples, and yellows. Slender radiating petals, one inner set surrounded by a larger one, give the effect of an opening rose.

> "The rose is beauty and love—the ideal of the virgin."
>
> —Allan Temko

In the center of the north rose, Mary is seated on a throne as she holds the Christ child. This window is dedicated to the Old Testament, with its petals decorated in images of Old Testament kings and prophets. The south rose, a gift of

OPPOSITE: *The north rose window shows Mary holding the Christ Child at the center with images of kings and prophets of the Old Testament surrounding them. Constructed in 1250, most of the original glasswork is still intact.*

King Louis IX and built in 1260, ten years after the north rose, contains eighty-four panels depicting New Testament figures. Considered the grandest of the three roses with its southern exposure that allows light to pour in throughout the day, the south rose features an image of Jesus at its center, seated on a throne with a lamb leaping at his feet.

Glass artisans used secret formulas to infuse cobalt, iron oxide, and silver oxides into molten glass to create varieties of blue, red, yellow, purple, brown, and green for all the windows of Notre-Dame de Paris. Sadly, very little of the original glass remains: the majestic blue and ruby windows of the nave and brilliant windows of the choir are nineteenth-century reproductions (except for one pane of the choir), and among the three roses, only the north window retains most of its original twelfth- and thirteenth-century glass.

Restoration of the glass in the 1800s by French architect Eugène Viollet-le-Duc (1814–79), who reproduced the originals as closely as possible, was not the last word on the stained glass legacy of the cathedral. In June 1965, the highest windows of the nave were replaced with modern originals whose colors harmonize with the rest of the windows so perfectly that many visitors do not even realize that they are abstract designs. In these twenty-four sets of windows by master glassmaker Jacques Le Chevallier (1896–1987), small irregular shapes flow vertically and horizontally without forming figures or symbols. When seen from below, these vibrant works create the impact that Le Chevallier sought in all of his sacred abstract art—to present its "inexhaustible richness of forms and colors [that are] deeply attuned to our sensibility."

ABOVE: *One of the stained glass windows created for the cathedral in 1965 by painter and master glassmaker Jacques Le Chevallier.* **OPPOSITE:** *Light shines through a blue-and-green stained glass window, highlighting the monument commissioned by Napoleon to honor Archbishop Jean-Baptiste de Belloy; it was sculpted by Louis-Pierre Deseine in 1802–8.* **FOLLOWING PAGES:** *Detail of the stained glass that surrounds the cathedral's apse.*

WITNESS TO HISTORY

2

REVOLUTIONARY CHANGE

During the nearly two hundred years of building Notre-Dame de Paris, the original plan underwent many changes. In the 1220s, for example, the upper wall was rebuilt to contain larger windows that transformed the structure from four stories to three, and from 1300 to 1350 chapels were added to the choir at the east end. More alterations would come throughout the centuries as raids, wars, revitalized interest, and fire made their mark on the cathedral at the heart of Paris.

The first attack on the cathedral came in the early years of the Huguenot (French Protestant) movement in sixteenth-century France. The crown tolerated the Huguenots until 1534, when anti-Catholic posters decrying the papal mass were disseminated in several major cities—one was even posted on the door of King Francis I's bedchamber. In 1540, the king issued an edict supporting persecution of the Huguenots, fomenting a period of unrest; in 1548, a Huguenot

PREVIOUS PAGES: *Detail from the painting* Procession of the Catholic League on the Place de Grève, *c. 1590, depicts militant Catholics in an armed procession during the final days of the Wars of Religion. Notre-Dame cathedral is clearly seen in the background.* **OPPOSITE:** One Morning at the Gates of the Louvre, *painted in 1880 by Édouard Debat-Ponsan, shows Catherine de' Medici (mother of King Charles IX, in black) calmly viewing the bodies of victims of the 1572 St. Bartholomew's Day massacre.*

uprising in Paris targeted Notre-Dame. Reformers like John Calvin (1509–64) considered Catholicism—with its images, relics, and elements of the Mass—a "false religion" that veered from "spiritual" worship.

The Huguenot crusade against Catholic "idolatry" included pillaging churches and cathedrals to destroy the art and sculpture within. While few details are known of the 1548 attack on Notre-Dame, historian Carlos Eire's description of early sixteenth-century Protestant raids in his book *War Against the Idols* (1986) gives a general idea: "Churches were sacked, images smashed and burned, relics destroyed, sanctuaries desecrated, altars overturned, and consecrated hosts fed to dogs and goats." The midcentury raid on Notre-Dame and others like it eventually led to a prolonged and deadly conflict known as the French Wars of Religion, which would rage from 1562 to 1598.

More transformations came to the cathedral during the reign of Louis XIV (1638–1715), when the Sun King pulled down the sculpture-laden rood screen that separated the choir from the nave, replaced stained glass windows with the clear glass that was fashionable at the time, and demolished the pillar in the central doorway to make room for carriages to enter in grand processions.

Sweeping devastation came with the French Revolution (1789–99), when the cathedral was looted, vandalized, and stripped of its function. Revolutionists waged a policy of dechristianization in the country, vowing to replace Catholicism with Enlightenment ideas; they ransacked, burned, and closed down churches and cathedrals across France and executed priests and nuns. In Paris, they removed Notre-Dame's bells and melted down all but one, Emmanuel, to make cannonballs.

The young profiteer and future social theorist Henri de Saint-Simon (1760–1825) schemed to buy the cathedral in order to melt down and sell the metal roof, but he was arrested before he could follow through with his plan. In his 2005 history of France, Alistair Horne writes that during the revolution, the cathedral "had escaped by a whisker—scheduled for destruction, its stones had actually been put up for auction." In 1793, a mob climbed up ladders to reach the Gallery of Kings on the western facade, slipped nooses around the twenty-eight statues of biblical kings (whom they mistook for French kings), and pulled them down to crash on the pavement below. Allan Temko wrote that the crowd cheered with each crash and then rushed to break apart the statues and throw the torsos in the

Seine. Twenty-one of the heads from these statues were discovered behind a wall in a Paris mansion in 1977 and are now displayed in the Musée de Cluny.

With the interior gutted, a stage set was brought in from the opera house in November 1793 for the Festival of Reason, in which an actress dressed in white sat upon a mountain to be revered as the Goddess of Reason. A cast of similarly white-dressed women danced and sang hymns to liberty while people filed in through portals now flanked by busts of enlightenment philosophers. The festival was not a mockery of Christianity, however, but instead an expression of the rational or "natural religion" held by the majority of those who supported the revolution. As deists, they rejected the "revealed religion," religion based on divine revelation rather than reason. "Deism rather than atheism prevailed among the majority of the revolutionists even in the Paris sections," wrote historian Charles Lyttle.

The revolutionists sought to remove the Catholic Church, which they believed had betrayed the people's liberty by holding so much power, land, and influence. A few months after the Festival of Reason, a new inscription on the facade of

ABOVE: *The Kings of Judah statue heads on display at the Musée de Cluny's inaugural exhibition in 1977; sculpted between 1200 and 1240, the heads were presumed lost for 181 years until they turned up—three miles from the cathedral—during the restoration of an old mansion.*

A LA PH

Notre-Dame read, "The French people recognize the Supreme Being and the immortality of the soul." The revolutionaries' new religion for France is best described by a few lines from a speech by revolutionary leader Maximilien de Robespierre (1758–94) at the Festival of the Supreme Being on June 8, 1794. The Supreme Being, Robespierre said,

> did not create kings to devour the human race. He did not create priests to harness us like brute beasts to the carriages of kings, and to give the world examples of baseness, pride, perfidy, avarice, debauchery, and falsehood. He created the universe to proclaim His power. He created men to help each other, to love each other, and to attain happiness by way of virtue.

Executed by fellow revolutionists for his part in the dreadful Reign of Terror, in which thousands of his political enemies were sent to the guillotine, Robespierre's vision of a new state religion was short lived. With the end of the revolution at the hands of the young general Napoleon Bonaparte (1769–1821), Notre-Dame was returned to the Catholic Church.

By then, the cathedral was being used for various quasi-religious services and as a wine house, but soon Napoleon would call upon his favorite set designers from the opera house to decorate the building inside and out for his coronation.

Napoleon's policies toward the Church were based on his belief that gaining "popular sovereignty" meant governing men "as the majority of them want to be governed." His first goal regarding religion was to reinstate Catholicism to appeal to popular sentiment. His second motive was about power. As historian William Roberts writes, Napoleon viewed the established Church as "one of the chief means of social control." For Napoleon, healing the rift between France and the pope would solidify his power by avoiding social unrest. Society, Napoleon said, "cannot exist without inequality of wealth, and inequality of wealth cannot exist

La fete de la Raison dans Notre-Dame de Paris le 10 Novembre 1793, *by Charles-Louis Müller (1878), depicts the Festival of Reason. By early 1794 most of the festival's supporters, who'd renamed Notre-Dame the "Temple of Reason," had been guillotined.*

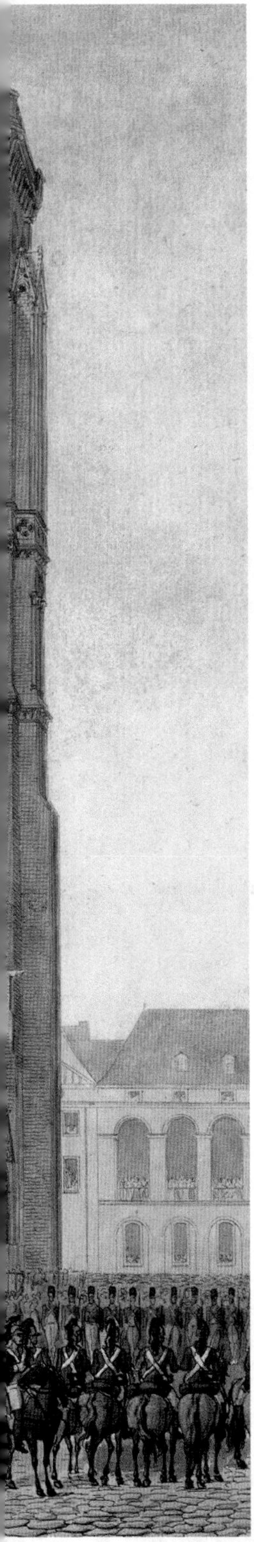

without religion. When a man is dying of hunger next to another who has plenty, it is impossible for him to accept this difference unless there is an authority that tells him: 'God wills it so.'"

Three years after reinstating Catholicism with the Concordat of 1801, Napoleon proclaimed himself emperor and chose Notre-Dame as the site of his lavish coronation. In a concession to Pope Pius VII, Napoleon and his wife, Joséphine—who had been married in a civil ceremony five years earlier—were married in a religious ceremony the night before the coronation. On coronation day, December 2, 1804, the cathedral was staged with a throne set on an elevated platform and its walls covered in tapestries. One observer wrote, "The church of Notre Dame was decorated with unequalled magnificence. Hangings of velvet, sprinkled with golden bees, descended from the roof to the pavement." We can assume that these hangings were an attempt to cover up the sad state of the cathedral. One clue about its regular appearance comes from the Duchess of Abrantès, who attended the event and referred to Notre-Dame as "that venerable pile" while describing the splendor of the coronation.

To light the interior, Napoleon's designers hung twenty-four chandeliers from the ceiling and attached gold candelabras to the pillars. The damaged floor was covered with rugs, and tiers of seats covered in silk and velvet were set up for the dignitaries. Outside, the broken-up western facade was hidden by an enormous columned pavilion built as a grand entrance. Attached to a long mast, a replica of the orange-red banner of Saint Denis flown in the Crusades waved above the entrance.

OPPOSITE: *This pen, ink, and watercolor drawing by Pierre-François-Léonard Fontaine depicts the back (east end) of Notre-Dame on December 2, 1804, as it appeared for Napoleon Bonaparte's coronation as emperor of France. The decorations and rotunda—set up to protect the most important guests from the weather as they got out of their coaches—were designed by Fontaine, the official government architect, and his partner, Charles Percier.* FOLLOWING PAGES: *Jacques-Louis David was commissioned by Napoleon to paint this huge canvas (20 × 32 feet [6.2 × 9 m])—* The Consecration of the Emperor Napoleon and the Coronation of Empress Joséphine on December 2, 1804*—to memorialize the splendor and convey the political power of this double coronation.*

Napoleon's infamous self-crowning was part of the formal sequence that had been planned to the last detail by a committee of French and papal officials. After being anointed by the pope and crowning himself, Napoleon placed a crown on Joséphine, France's new empress. The triumphant, grandiose music for two choirs and two orchestras, commissioned for the event, reverberated through the space and featured star performers of the day, such as violinist Rodolphe Kreutzer (to whom Beethoven would dedicate his famed ninth violin sonata) and Paris Opéra diva Alexandrine-Caroline Branchu.

For all the window dressing that made Notre-Dame a worthy spectacle for Napoleon's coronation, the cathedral had to wait another forty years for a revitalization plan dedicated to returning it to its former glory. The cathedral is indebted to novelist Victor Hugo, who sparked the new wave of public adoration for the crumbling building in the 1830s. Hugo's blockbuster novel of 1831, *Notre-Dame de Paris*, better known in English as *The Hunchback of Notre-Dame*, was as much a tribute to the cathedral as it was a grand melodrama of medieval Paris. As Hugo biographer Jean-Marc Hovasse explains, however, Hugo's admiration of the cathedral stopped at its Gothic artistry: "The book has lost none of its virulent protest against the dead weight with which religion, in the broadest sense, burdens societies—with women and justice invariably the first victims." In stark irony, the novel that offended the Vatican saved the cathedral.

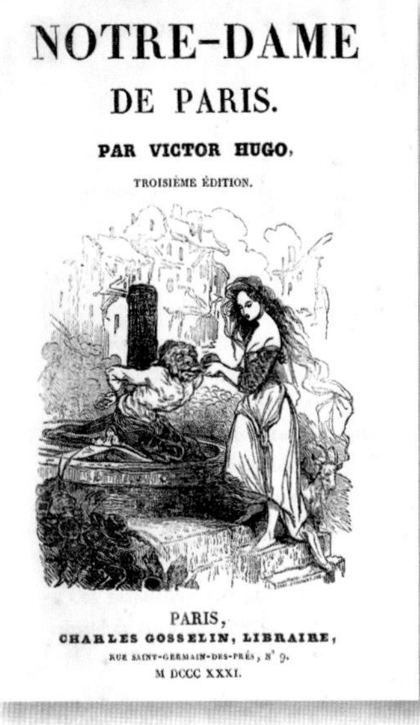
NOTRE-DAME
DE PARIS.
PAR VICTOR HUGO,
TROISIÈME ÉDITION.
PARIS,
CHARLES GOSSELIN, LIBRAIRE,
RUE SAINT-GERMAIN-DES-PRÉS, N° 9.
M DCCC XXXI.

The story of Quasimodo, the deformed hunchback bellringer of Notre-Dame, his beloved gypsy girl Esmeralda, and archdeacon Frollo is a romantic tragedy that includes two chapters devoted solely to the cathedral. The novel created a public demand for the cathedral's restoration, and in 1841, the newly formed Commission on Historical Monuments appointed architects Eugène Viollet-le-Duc and Jean-Baptiste Lassus (1807–57) to do the job. Viollet-le-Duc, passionate about Gothic architecture, had already worked on Gothic restorations and would spend nearly

OPPOSITE: *Chromolithograph frontispiece to* The Esmeralda Waltzes *by William Sharp, c. 1840–1849, showing the gypsy Esmeralda dancing with her pet goat.* **ABOVE:** *Title page of the third edition of Victor Hugo's* Notre-Dame de Paris, *1831.*

twenty years bringing Notre-Dame back to life. The work took place from 1845 to 1864, with Viollet-le-Duc carrying on alone after the death of Lassus in 1857.

Paris chose Notre-Dame as one of its first restorations because it was the ideal symbol of the Romantic movement. The French were interested in everything indigenous to France, and the cathedral was "a focal point for interest in local history, life in mediaeval France, and in all the monuments of France's past," writes historian Daniel D. Reiff.

The Notre-Dame we see today carries Viollet-le-Duc's distinct mark of renovation style. While his writings promoted a restoration process that stayed faithful to the original and the specific changes made in subsequent centuries, he could not always refrain from filling in the blanks with his own touches. His controversial

OPPOSITE: *The copper statue of the apostle St. Thomas (with the face of architect and Notre-Dame master restorer, Viollet-le-Duc) on the roof of the cathedral, November 30, 2012.* **ABOVE:** *A photograph of the south side of Notre-Dame, c. 1852–53, taken by Édouard Baldus before the new spire was created.*

decisions included the replacement of the thirteenth-century spire, which had been removed during the revolution, with a more contemporary design. Climbing up from its base are twelve-foot- (3.6 m) tall copper sculptures of the twelve disciples and four evangelists—additions that were purely le-Duc's idea rather than replacements of pieces that had once appeared on the cathedral. These figures include Viollet-le-Duc's signature in the form of Saint Thomas crafted to resemble himself (see photograph on page 56). He also commissioned fifty-four chimera, decorative sculptures perched on the balcony that connects the north and south bell towers. Fantastical figures peering over the city, the chimera take the shape of mythical

ABOVE: *The Angel of the Resurrection on the roof of Notre-Dame photographed by Charles Marville, c. 1860.* **OPPOSITE:** *Notre-Dame de Paris photographed in the early 1860s by Charles Soulier, showing the new spire shortly after its recreation during the restoration by Viollet-le-Duc.*

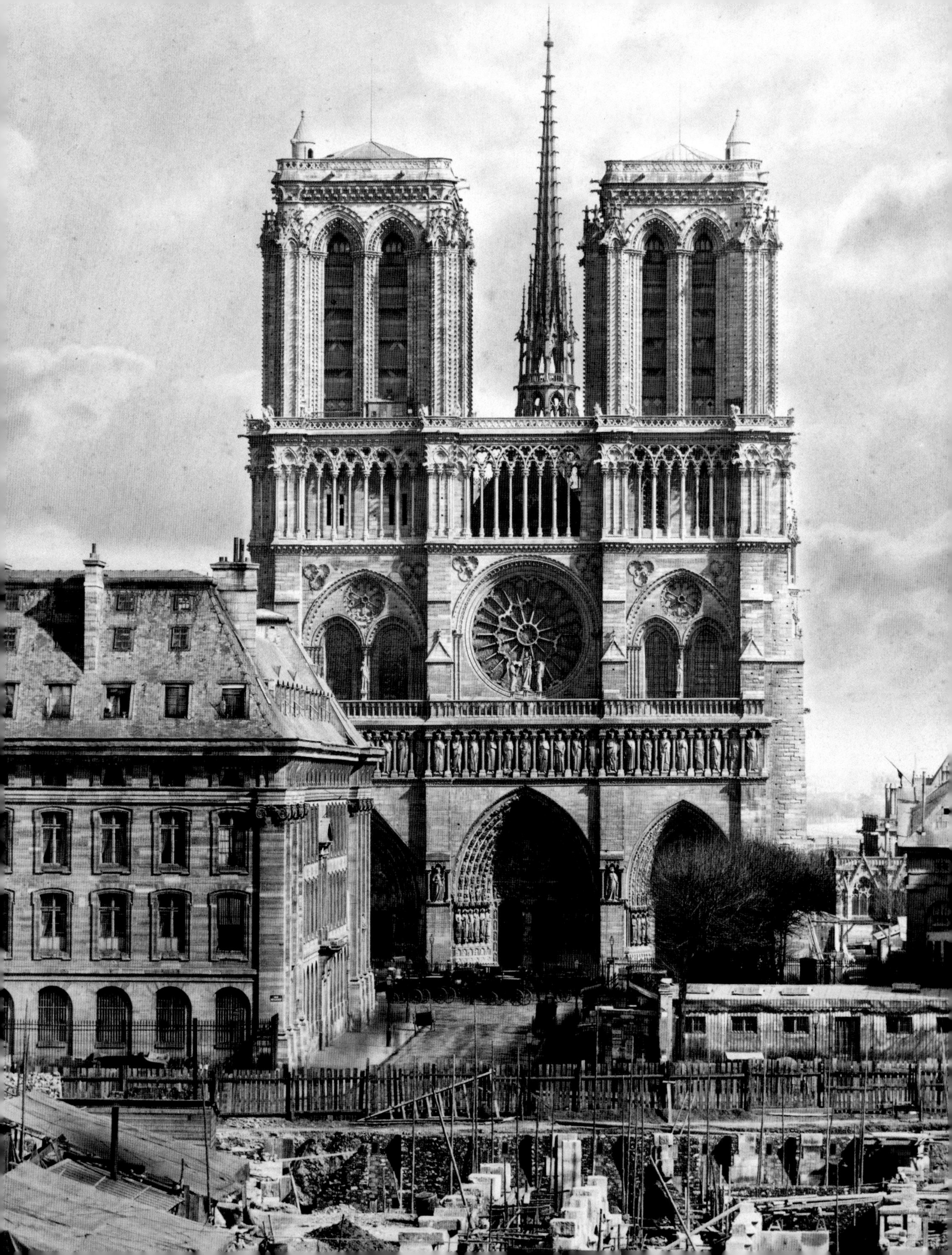

creatures, bizarre hybrids, and frightening animals. Viollet-le-Duc was inspired by Quasimodo in his design of the horned and winged Stryga or Strix chimera, which rests its head in its hands and sticks out its tongue (see illustration on page 71).

Viollet-le-Duc's work inside and out included building a new sacristy, where the vestments and sacred vessels are kept; rebuilding the south rose window, which had been heavily damaged during the revolution; and replacing more than sixty statues missing from the western facade. Based on Viollet-le-Duc's research of statues from cathedrals built at roughly the same time as Notre-Dame de Paris, chief sculptor Adolphe-Victor Geoffroy-Dechaume (1816–92) and his assistants copied the medieval pieces as closely as possible. At the same time, Viollet-le-Duc commissioned Aristide Cavaillé-Coll (1811–99) to build a new symphonic organ, another jewel of French romanticism.

Archbishop Georges Darboy led the dedication of the restored cathedral on May 31, 1864. While debate over Viollet-le-Duc's restoration seems endless, the sheer scope and complexity of his task at Notre-Dame de Paris has made him a legend of French history, architecture, and culture.

During the rule of Napoleon III in the Second French Empire, Baron Georges-Eugène Haussmann (1809–91) redesigned Paris in one of the largest urban planning projects in history. To bring the still-medieval city into the modern era, he widened streets, built grand boulevards, refined neoclassical apartment buildings, divided the city into arrondissements (districts), designed a new sewer system, and created four large parks.

Haussmann's twenty-year transformation of the city also cleared a large section of Île de la Cité to create breathing space for Notre-Dame. Its small parvis, or square, was expanded (see foreground of photograph on page 59) by tearing down homes and the Hôtel-Dieu, a massive seventh-century hospital, which was rebuilt on the opposite side of the enlarged parvis across from the cathedral. With plenty of room to now stand back and behold the cathedral, the layout renewed the identity of the cathedral as one of the great attractions of the city and of Europe.

OPPOSITE: *Photograph by Charles Marville, c. 1860, showing the new spire and the Île Saint-Louis in the background.* FOLLOWING PAGES: *Bronze figures of the apostles surround the spire of Notre-Dame, June 2016.*

Reading the Cathedral

Built at a time when the majority of the people were illiterate, Notre-Dame de Paris tells the stories of the Old and New Testaments through images in stone, wood, and glass. The statues on the western facade and within every portal, wood carvings on the choir wall, and stained glass windows all tell stories that connected the community in their faith.

The triangular tympana above each of the three sets of wooden doors on the western facade contain carvings to be read from bottom to top. To the left is the Portal of the Virgin, on which the bottom level shows the Old Testament prophets holding scrolls that prophesy Christ. Above that, Mary is shown on her deathbed surrounded by Jesus and the twelve disciples. Angels at her head and feet wait to carry her up to heaven. At the top, Mary is crowned the Queen of Heaven.

Above the center doorway, the scene in the Portal of Judgment (opposite), the scene begins with the dead rising from their graves on the bottom level. Next, those being sent to heaven are being led to the left, while those condemned to hell are being pushed by a demon to the right. In the final section at the top, the risen Christ is seated between the Virgin Mary and Saint John.

The Portal of Saint Anne on the right depicts the marriages of Anne and Joachim (the Virgin Mary's parents) and Mary and Joseph. The center section shows more episodes of the Virgin Mary's life—the Annunciation, the Visitation, the birth of Jesus, and the Adoration of the Magi. Above this is Mary wearing a crown, seated with the child Jesus in her lap.

On the north side of the cathedral, the Cloister Portal also contains three levels. The lowest section contains scenes from Jesus's life, including his birth and presentation at the temple. The two levels above tell the story of Theophilus of Adana, a sixth-century cleric who made a contract with the devil and afterward prayed to Mary for help. She took the contract from the devil, who is seen crouching before her, and freed the bishop's soul. The top section shows the bishop of Adana telling the story to rapt listeners and holding up the devil's contract.

On the opposite side of the cathedral, the Saint Stephen Portal tells the story of Christianity's first martyr. In the lower panel, Stephen discusses theology with

OPPOSITE: *Close-up view of the Portal of Judgment at Notre-Dame cathedral, April 2013.*

rabbis and commoners. Above this are dramatic scenes of his death by stoning and his burial, and at the top, figures of Christ, and two angels waiting for his soul.

Inside the cathedral, the choir wall contains bas-relief masterpieces carved from 1300 to 1350, still retaining their vibrant colors, that portray the life of Christ. The north panels show scenes from Mary's life and the story of Jesus from his childhood to the Last Supper, and his praying in the garden of Gethsemane. The middle section of the wall is no longer in the cathedral, but the south wall portrays Christ after his resurrection, appearing to Mary Magdalene and the disciples.

The cathedral's rose windows, as described on pages 37–38, communicate through color and symbol, as do many of the tall stained glass panels throughout the nave and choir. All of the panels are works from the nineteenth century and later, including the set inside the sacristy. The sacristy windows by artist Alfred Gerente (1821–68) tell the story of Saint Genevieve, a patron saint of Paris, whose prayers were said to fend off the Huns in the fifth century.

ABOVE: *Jesus's appearance to the apostles in the upper room (left) and to Thomas (right) are shown in this detail of the fourteenth-century wooden panels on the choir wall.* OPPOSITE: *Photograph, attributed to Bisson Frères, of Saint Stephen's portal on the south transept, c. 1850–1865.* FOLLOWING PAGES: *Detail of the Neo-Gothic Portal of Judgment showing the tortures of the damned. This was restored by Eugène Viollet-le-Duc and Jean-Baptiste Lassus in the 1840s.*

1003, Paris Notre Dame

Gargoyles and Chimeras

The fantastical creatures sculpted across the exterior of Notre-Dame de Paris have fascinated visitors ever since they were restored in the mid-1800s. Two kinds of "grotesques" appear on the cathedral: the gargoyles, which serve a function as drainage pipes, and the chimeras, which are decorative pieces only. Both were created by sculptor Victor Pyanet during Viollet-le-Duc's restoration of the cathedral from 1845 to 1864.

Hundreds of gargoyles stick out from the upper sections of the cathedral to shoot rainwater away from the walls, holding the water in their long necks and ejecting it from their mouths. These fierce-looking objects deteriorate easily and often need to be replaced. Today's gargoyles are cracking, crumbling, and falling. The fifty-four chimeras, gazing down at the city from the colonnade between the two towers, take the form of animals, hybrid creatures with horns and wings, and hooded human-like characters. Some perch on the stone balustrade while others sprout from it, revealing only the upper part of their bodies.

Restorer Viollet-le-Duc wrote that the west side of the cathedral originally held "enormous sculpted beasts, which standing out against the sky, give life to these masses of stone." In medieval France, many believed that gargoyles and chimera represented evil spirits that had been cast out of the cathedral and remained on the exterior to protect it. One medieval legend explains the origins of the gargoyles in a story of about Saint Romanus,

OPPOSITE: *Close-up photograph of a chimera taken about 1870.*
RIGHT: *An 1853 etching by Charles Méryon of "Le Styrge" (the vampire), one of the most famous grotesques that were added during the Viollet-le-Duc restoration of the cathedral. Méryon had written the couplet "The insatiable Vampire, eternal lust / forever coveting its food in the great city" on earlier versions of the print.*

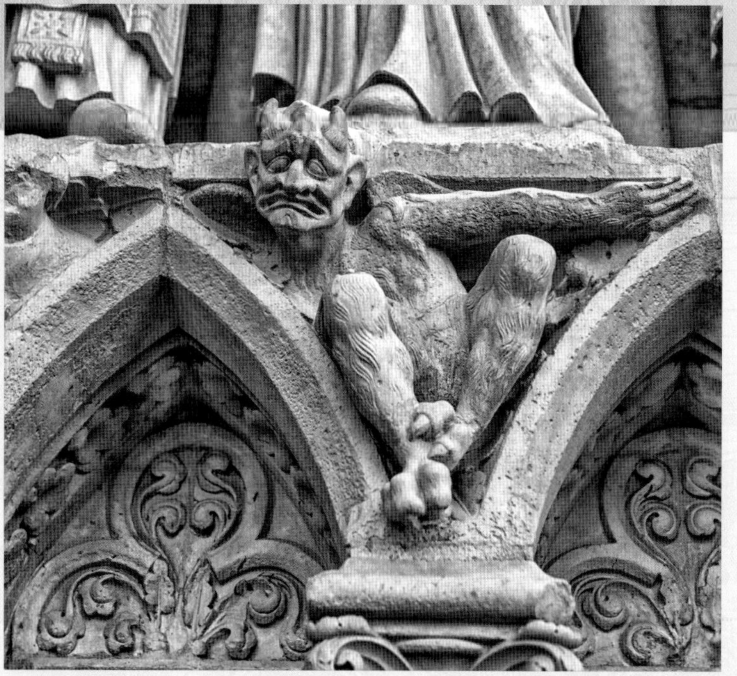

the seventh-century bishop of Rouen. After capturing the fire-breathing dragon known as Gargouille, who was terrorizing the city, Saint Romanus brought the beast back to Rouen to be burned. The fiery nature of the dragon's head and neck prevented those parts from burning, and this is where the gargoyle water spouts took their name. Sculptors took the dragon monster as their design "to emit cold water as a perennial jeer and flout against the creature that seared men with his red-hot exhalations," as one writer explained in an architectural journal in 1906.

The mystery and playfulness of Notre-Dame's gargoyles and chimera have inspired some of the most popular photographs of the cathedral and ignited various ideas about their meaning. Art scholar Michael Camille has described the reconstructed chimeras as reflections of society's ideas at the time, from debates over evolution and race to attitudes about the working class and the clergy.

ABOVE: *Detail of a creature found at the Portal of the Virgin just beneath Saint Genevieve.* **OPPOSITE:** *This 1930 photograph by Marcel Fleureau titled* Cathédrale Notre-Dame, Galerie des chimères, Balustrade, côté est, *shows the east bell tower with several fanciful animal chimera, a water-spout gargoyle at the bottom left, and the Angel of the Resurrection in the foreground.*

Cy commence le vi^e. livre Lequel contient en soy. xlv. Chapittres.
Du premier desquelz il commence a parler de la venue du jeune roy henry dangleterre a paris ou il fut couronne a roy de France. Chapittre. i.

Apres la mort de ce tres noble roy henry dangleterre v^e. de ce nom regna son filz henry. vi^e. Lequel en leage de huit ans passa la mer et vint descendre a Callaix Et de la il sen alla a Rouen en northmandie ou il seiourna une espace de temps Et puis sen alla a pontoise qui fut environ a lissue du mois de novembre Lan mil quatre cens et trente Et de

A World Stage

With a few exceptions, Notre-Dame de Paris did not become the scene of France's historic ceremonies until the First Empire, which began with Napoleon Bonaparte's coronation in 1804. Until then, most kings were traditionally coronated at Notre-Dame de Reims, and their funerals and burials were held at the basilica of Saint-Denis near Paris. The cathedral did, however, host a number of majestic events in its first few centuries, which put it at the center of these historic events.

King Henry VI of England was crowned king of France in the cathedral on December 16, 1431, inheriting the throne after the death of Henry V of England. Ten-year-old Henry VI was the only monarch ever crowned king of both England and France, and the cathedral, decorated in gold draperies, was filled with music sung by the combined choirs of the English Chapel Royal and Notre-Dame de Paris.

Royal weddings of the sixteenth century in the cathedral began with James V of Scotland and Madeleine de Valois, who were married in January 1537. This tragically short marriage ended with the death of the sixteen-year-old princess just two months after she and James V returned to Scotland.

The most famous wedding at Notre-Dame took place on April 24, 1558, when Mary Stuart, Queen of Scots, age seventeen, married Francis de Valois, age fifteen and heir to the French throne. A commentary about the wedding published at the time described the pomp surrounding the official procession into the cathedral:

> The brilliant ceremony took place in the morning at the Gothic cathedral of Notre Dame which had been elaborately decorated in honor of the royal couple. Great crowds assembled in the streets to witness the colorful wedding procession to the cathedral. In the presence of royalty, prelates of the Church,

OPPOSITE: *This illuminated manuscript page from the fifteenth-century volume 5 of* Anciennes chroniques d'Angleterre *by Jean de Wavrin shows ten-year-old Henry VI being coronated as king of France in Notre-Dame Cathedral in 1431.* ABOVE: *Portrait of Mary Stuart, Queen of Scots, with her first husband, Francis II, King of France, c. 1559.* FOLLOWING PAGES: *An eighteenth-century engraving depicting the nave of Notre-Dame Cathedral as Marie Antoinette arrives to attend mass for the birth of her son, the future Louis XVII, in 1781.*

> princes of the blood, exalted members of the aristocracy, and high city officials, the dynasties of Stuart and Valois were joined together in a matrimonial alliance.... Before the great door of the church a royal canopy was erected covered with fleurs de lys with tapestry of similar nature on the two sides of the door.... And, from ten to eleven o'clock in the morning came first the Swiss, dressed in their liveries, carrying their halberds, with their tambourines and fifes performing according to their custom for about half an hour.

The writer described Mary's wedding gown as "a garment white as a lily and so sumptuously and richly made that it would be impossible to describe it and of which two young ladies carried a wonderfully long train."

Fourteen years later, a wedding with tragic consequences took place at the cathedral. Marguerite de Valois and Henri de Navarre, a Protestant, were forced

OPPOSITE: *An 1842 lithograph of the funeral service for the Duke of Orléans in Notre-Dame Cathedral by Courtin and Grenier de Saint Martin.* ABOVE: *Lithograph of the state funeral of Louis Pasteur at Notre-Dame Cathedral by C. Hentschel, c. 1895.*

to marry in an attempt to end the religious wars between the Catholics and Huguenots. The highly disputed wedding took place on August 18, 1572; four days later, a major Huguenot leader was shot in an attempted assassination, further stoking tensions and leading King Charles IX to order the killing of all the Huguenots in the city. The cathedral's royal wedding of 1572 will always be associated with the St. Bartholomew's Day Massacre, which ignited France's so-called fourth war of religion.

One of the most eminent religious ceremonies at the cathedral in modern times took place in July 1909, when Pope Pius X beatified France's fifteenth-century

ABOVE: *Crowds gathering outside Notre-Dame de Paris for French president Charles de Gaulle's memorial service, November 12, 1970.* OPPOSITE: *Pope John Paul II, center, celebrating the beatification mass for Frédéric Ozanam, the nineteenth-century French layman who founded the Saint Vincent de Paul charity, August 22, 1997.*

heroine Joan of Arc. Charles Desvergnes sculpted a statue of Saint Joan for the cathedral in 1920, when Parisian families were praying to the saint as they mourned the loss of their loved ones in World War I.

The cathedral took center stage after the liberation of Paris in World War II as the site of a thanksgiving service attended by the triumphant French general Charles de Gaulle on August 26, 1944. Amid random sniper fire, the general inspired the attendees to calmly stand for the Te Deum, the Catholic hymn traditionally sung to give thanks on momentous occasions. As one British journalist remarked, de Gaulle's bravery within the iconic cathedral increased his status even more: "Even his enemies now knew," said Aidan Crawley, "that spiritually de Gaulle was master of France."

More recently, the cathedral has conducted requiem masses to commemorate world leaders after their deaths, including General Charles de Gaulle in November 1970, President François Mitterrand in January 1996, and Pope John Paul II in April 2005.

Throughout the entire year of 2013, Notre-Dame pulled out all the stops to honor one of France's most beloved icons: the cathedral itself. To celebrate its 850th anniversary, Notre-Dame de Paris installed new bells (see page 129), held musical performances and seminars, and welcomed even larger numbers of visitors from throughout the world.

WORLD WARS

In October 1914, less than three months after Germany declared war on France, a German plane bombed the cathedral. In November, a medical correspondent in Paris wrote, "Quite recently one of the enemy's aeroplanes also contrived to drop a bomb on Notre Dame de Paris, though fortunately the damage done was insignificant, a slight tear in the roofing." The cathedral was spared any serious harm in World War I, but by the war's end, 1.3 million French soldiers had died, and 1 million more were wounded in action.

The cathedral also survived World War II, its facade covered in sandbags. The threat of its destruction was imminent, however, in the last days of the German occupation. Hitler ordered his military leader in Paris, General Dietrich von Choltitz, to destroy the city, including its monuments, before the Allies arrived. The order from headquarters is said to have read, "Paris is to be transformed into a pile of rubble. The commanding general must defend the city to the last man and should die, if necessary, under the ruins." In his memoir (which some historians dispute), Choltitz relayed a phone call he claimed to have had with a German chief of staff about how he would follow out the order:

"I thank you for your excellent order."

"Which order, General?"

A tank on Notre-Dame square during the liberation of Paris, August 1944.

"The demolition order, of course. Here's what I've done: I've had three tons of explosives brought into Notre-Dame, two tons into the Invalides, a ton into the Chambre des deputes. I'm just about to order that the Arc de Triomphe be blown up to provide a clear line of fire."

Choltitz explained that the call was meant to convey the ridiculousness of the order, which he supposedly never intended to carry out, and he proceeded to evacuate some of the remaining German forces in secret. He surrendered on August 25, 1944, when the French 2nd Armored Division and the US 4th Infantry Division liberated the city. The next day, French soldiers, tanks, and General Charles de Gaulle paraded down the Champs-Élysées toward Notre-Dame, where a service would commemorate the city's liberation. (Writer Simone de Beauvoir described the parade as more of "a popular carnival, disorganized and magnificent.") Just as the general strode across the square in front of the cathedral, snipers, perhaps Germans, opened fire. An American eyewitness described the scene:

> The air crackled into life with bullets, hissing and whining all over the square. The French light tanks began firing over our heads at some Germans across the Seine. Germans were also shooting from Notre Dame and from nearby houses. For twenty-five minutes [we] lay on our stomachs crouched beside the jeep. We could see no likely shelter of any kind. There was so much shooting that we could hardly hear one another speak. Guns, machine guns, rifles—everything was going off together in one great ear-splitting, crackling inferno of sound. . . . I could see the sun glint on the white marks where the bullets had struck Norte Dame.

Other than those nicks, the cathedral miraculously survived the war and four years of Nazi occupation. At the thanksgiving service, de Gaulle took his place of honor in the cathedral to commemorate the liberation, and the short but reverent service included the fitting performance of an arrangement of the Magnificat, the canticle of Mary found in Luke 1:

My soul magnifies the Lord. / And my spirit leaps for joy in God my Savior.

OPPOSITE: *Photograph showing the roof of Notre-Dame after being struck by a German bomb in October 1914.* **FOLLOWING PAGES:** *Sandbags stacked against Notre-Dame Cathedral, c. 1916.*

PARIS - ROOF ON NOTRE DAME STRUCK BY BOMB 3277-5

GLACES
-Choco
GLACES

OPPOSITE: *American servicemen buying ice cream from a stall outside the cathedral after the liberation of Paris, August 1944.* ABOVE: *French general Philippe François Marie Leclerc de Hauteclocque (with cane) in a motorcade passing in front of Notre-Dame during the liberation of Paris, August 1944.*

ABOVE and OPPOSITE: *"Dame de Coeur," a twenty-minute sound and video projection spectacular created by director Bruno Seillier, ran between November 7 and 11, 2017, marking the hundredth anniversary of World War I and celebrating the survival of the cathedral through revolutions, rioting, vandals, and two world wars.*

ZERO DES ROUTES DE FRANCE

THE PEOPLE'S CATHEDRAL 3

TIMELESS AND CONTEMPORARY

Like French Gothic architecture itself, Notre-Dame de Paris is a synthesis of function and beauty. As historic as the cathedral is, it still operates as a church for the city of Paris and its visitors. Catholics attend daily masses and the main celebrations of the church year in the nave where worshippers have gathered for nearly 860 years. Paris has been a diocese (district or territory) of the Roman Catholic Church since c. 250 CE, and as one of ninety-nine dioceses in France, the city is a metropolitan archdiocese with its seat at Notre-Dame. The current archbishop, Michel Aupetit, has led the archdiocese since 2017 from his official residence on rue Barbet-de-Jouy.

Before the fire of April 15, 2019, the cathedral conducted seven masses in French on Sundays, including a Gregorian Mass featuring Gregorian chant and vespers (evening prayer) service. The archbishop traditionally presided over the last Mass of the day, which came after vespers, and the rest of the week, Mass was celebrated at noon and after vespers.

The work of running the cathedral includes clergy as well as dozens of lay staff and volunteers, including priests (ten in service in 2019),

PREVIOUS PAGES: *The central nave of the Gothic cathedral, July 2017.*
OPPOSITE: *After 850 years, Notre-Dame de Paris is still the heart of the city.*

"Medieval people knew—perhaps more vividly than we—that human life is a dangerous proposition. . . . When pilgrims enter the hull of this cathedral-ship, they are meant to feel a rush of relief, a keen sensation of being secure even as the waves crash against the vessel."

—ROBERT BARRON, *HEAVEN IN STONE AND GLASS*, 2000

altar servers, accountants, secretaries, sacristans who prepare the objects for the Mass, technical staff, a printer, event managers, organists, singers, and the keeper of the keys.

Victor Hugo would be astonished to know just how popular Quasimodo's cathedral has become. Thirteen million people—worshippers, religious pilgrims, and tourists—walk through its portals every year. An estimated fifty thousand come through on its busiest days. The heartiest of them trek up the towers (each a total of 387 steps) to inspect the chimeras and the view, starting with a trip up the north tower stairway to reach the Gallery of the Chimeras. At the other end of the Gallery, the hike up the south tower is rewarded with another breathtaking view of Paris sprawling outward from its heart, where the cathedral stands.

Allan Temko described the cathedral as alive, a building that "moves, breathes, aspires to Heaven with a human impulse." A variety of impulses brings many people to walk Notre-Dame's aisles daily, a distraction that can be discomforting to those who simply come to pray. But the cathedral manages to be what it needs to be for each type of visitor. "The cathedral has incarnated in the eyes of its visitors, throughout history, multiple and intertwined meanings," writes historian Évelyne Cohen. "In their great diversity, tourists, visitors, and faithful make Notre-Dame de Paris the monument most visited by our contemporaries."

OPPOSITE: *Cardinal Vingt-Trois (foreground, center) leads a pontifical Mass at Notre-Dame commencing the year-long celebrations marking the 850th anniversary of its founding, December 12, 2012.* **FOLLOWING PAGES:** *Easter vigil in Notre-Dame, April 7, 2012.*

1951

OPPOSITE: *Photographer and famed postcard editor Albert Monier's image* Conciliabule de religieuses devant Notre-Dame, *1950.* **ABOVE:** *Painters at the River Seine with Notre-Dame in the background, 1929.*

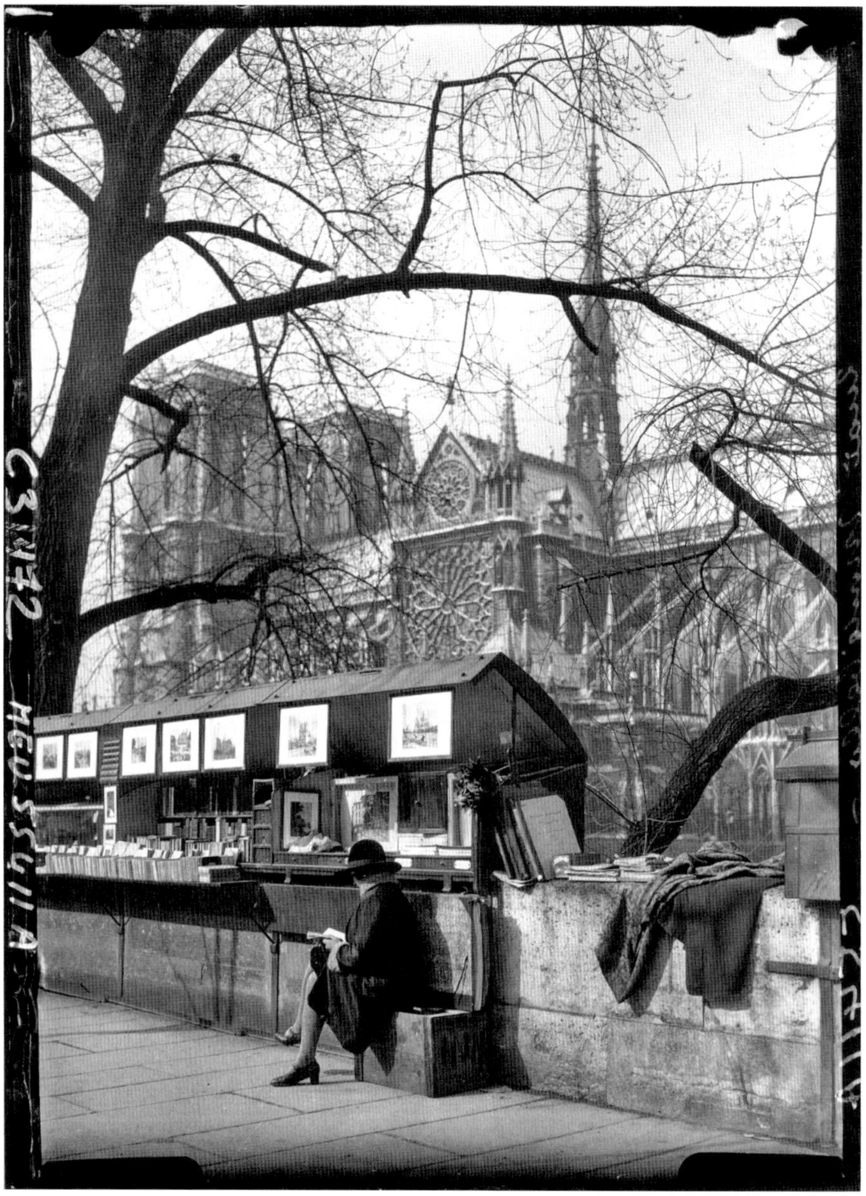

ABOVE: *A press image by Agence Meurisse of Notre-Dame taken from the Quai de Montebello with print merchants in the forground, 1928.* OPPOSITE: *An undated color etching by twentieth-century printmaker Hans Figura titled* Notre Dame I, Bookstalls.

HANS
FIGURA

The Concierge of Notre Dame

From The Secret Paris of the 30s, *Brassaï*

One winter day in 1932, I got the urge to climb to the top of Notre-Dame at night.

"The concierge is on the second floor," they told me at the entrance. So I climbed up—200 steps—and between two groups of tourists, I confronted the woman who watched over Notre-Dame.

"Climb up here at night, sir? It's unheard of! It's out of the question. We're a national museum, just like the Louvre. And we close at five!" I discreetly slipped her a bill.

"I shouldn't let you, sir! It's wrong! Even though I am very badly paid . . . and I have heart trouble, and I'm short of breath . . . Imagine! Two hundred steps every time I come up, and such steps! I was young once, not so fat, and I climbed up here twice a day. Now I come up in the morning and bring my lunch, and I don't go back until evening . . . Coming up here twice in one day will be hard on me, very hard. But you're generous, and you love Notre-Dame! I'll do it for you . . . a favor I've never done for anyone else . . . Only promise me not to use any light, not even a match. We're right across from the Préfecture de Police. The slightest glimmer would be suspicious. I could lose my job over it . . ."

I reassure her. Taking advantage of a lull while the tourists moved off, the capacious woman continued in a low voice: "Look." With her plump finger, she indicated a particular place down in the square. "You see the third lamppost on the right? Be there at ten tonight. I don't want you to come looking for me in the concierge's loge."

I was under the lamppost on the stroke of ten, and through the November mist, I saw a voluminous silhouette emerge from the Rue du Cloître-Notre-Dame and come toward me.

"Follow me," the concierge whispered in a muffled voice.

We were like conspirators in a Victor Hugo novel. She carried a bunch of keys, and with them she opened the heavy door.

We climbed the spiral staircase. It was totally dark; the climb lasted an eternity. At last, we reached the open platform. Completely out of breath, my accomplice collapsed into her chair. Impatient, enraptured, I ran beside the balustrade. It was more beautiful than I had imagined! The dark, indefinable shapes were black as night, the fog over Paris was milk white! Scarcely discernible, the Hôtel-Dieu, the Tour Saint-Jacques, the Quartier Latin, the Sorbonne, were luminous and somber shapes . . . Paris was ageless, bodiless . . . Present and past, history and legend, intermingled. Atop this cathedral, I expected to meet Quasimodo the bell-ringer around some corner, and later, upon descending into the city, I would certainly pass Verlaine and François Villon, the Marquis de Sade, Gérard de Nerval, Restif de la Bretonne.

"It's marvelous, marvelous," I kept exclaiming to myself.

"Isn't it, sir?" the fat woman replied, brimming with pride at being the concierge of Notre-Dame. "You don't see that anywhere else . . . We're at the heart of Paris . . . It beats the Eiffel Tower, doesn't it?"

But I had to get to the very top.

"Climb on up if you want, sir. I'll stay here; I can't go any farther . . . I trust you. Go on. You won't steal the towers of Notre-Dame."

So up I climbed, still in complete darkness. I mounted the 387 steps. Coming out at the top, I saw behind the cathedral's spire the Seine glittering like a curved sword. Suddenly my foot brushed against something soft. I bent down, and beneath my fingers, numb from the cold of that November night, I felt the feathers of a dead pigeon. A dead pigeon, still warm . . .

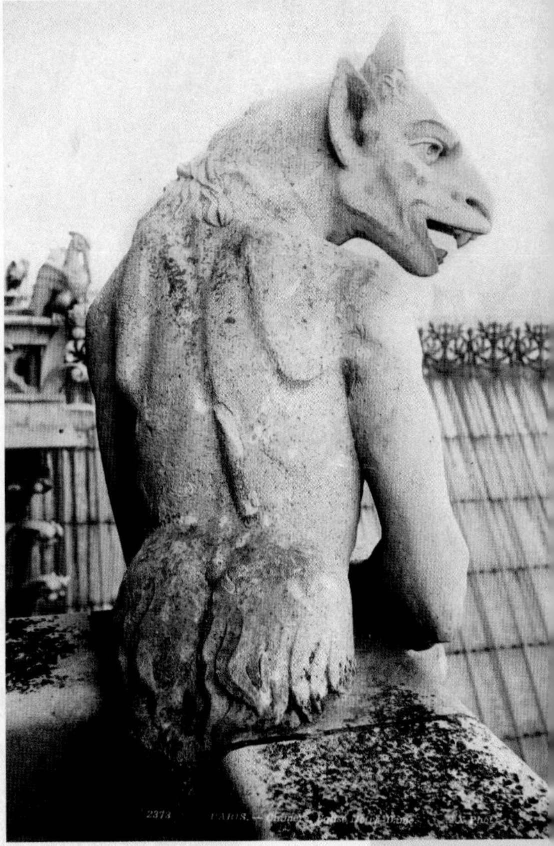

Unattributed photograph of a chimera, Notre-Dame, c. 1880s.

"There are no tourists in Notre-Dame, because this term . . . does not do justice to the mystery that drives humanity to seek something beyond itself."

—MICHEL AUPETIT, ARCHBISHOP OF PARIS

OPPOSITE: *Louis Armand, the chief guardian of Notre-Dame in 1968, poses with some (but not all) of his keys outside the south tower beside a stone bird.* ABOVE: *Tourists at the cathedral in the 1950s.* FOLLOWING PAGES: *This image of specialists cleaning the figure of Jesus on the Portal of Judgment tympanum, May 1963, gives a sense of the scale of the portal's sculptures.*

The Cathedral at the Movies

As one of the most iconic historic sites in the world, Notre-Dame de Paris has appeared in dozens of films from silent era gems to animated Hollywood blockbusters. At least thirteen movies have been based on Victor Hugo's classic novel alone, from the 1905 French silent short film *Esmeralda* to the 1996 Disney animated musical *The Hunchback of Notre Dame*, starring the voices of Demi Moore and Tom Hulce. An early Hollywood version of *The Hunchback of Notre Dame* from 1939 starred Maureen O'Hara and Charles Laughton, and in the 1999 French comedy *Quasimodo d'El Paris*, a modern-day Quasimodo is accused of a string of murders.

In the 2015 documentary *The Walk*, French performer Philippe Petit walks a tightrope between the cathedral's two towers in 1971 before taking on the same feat between the World Trade Center towers in New York City in 1974. Action movies that take their battles to the roof include director Paul Anderson's 2011 *The Three Musketeers* and Stephen Sommers's 2004 *Van Helsing*. Among the romantic films featuring Notre-Dame de Paris as a backdrop are the classic musical *An American in Paris* (1951) with dancers Gene Kelly and Leslie Caron, *Secret People* (1952) with Audrey Hepburn, and *Before Sunset* (2004), starring Ethan Hawke and Julie Delpy. The cathedral also shows up in animated films such as Disney's *The Aristocats* (1970); *Ratatouille*, the 2007 Academy Award–winning hit from Pixar Animation Studios; *Rugrats in Paris: The Movie* (2000); and *Cars 2* (2011), in which the cathedral sports "car-goyle" statues and exhaust-pipe flying buttresses.

The cathedral is the setting of a critical plotline in Jean-Pierre Jeunet's *Amélie* (2001), starring Audrey Tautou as the shy Parisian waitress who conjures up magical adventures. Forty years earlier, stylish thrillers such as Jean-Luc Godard's *Breathless* (1960) and Stanley Donen's *Charade* (1963) with Audrey Hepburn and Cary Grant included images of the cathedral as part of the Paris milieu.

OPPOSITE: The Hunchback of Notre-Dame *Belgian movie poster, 1923.*

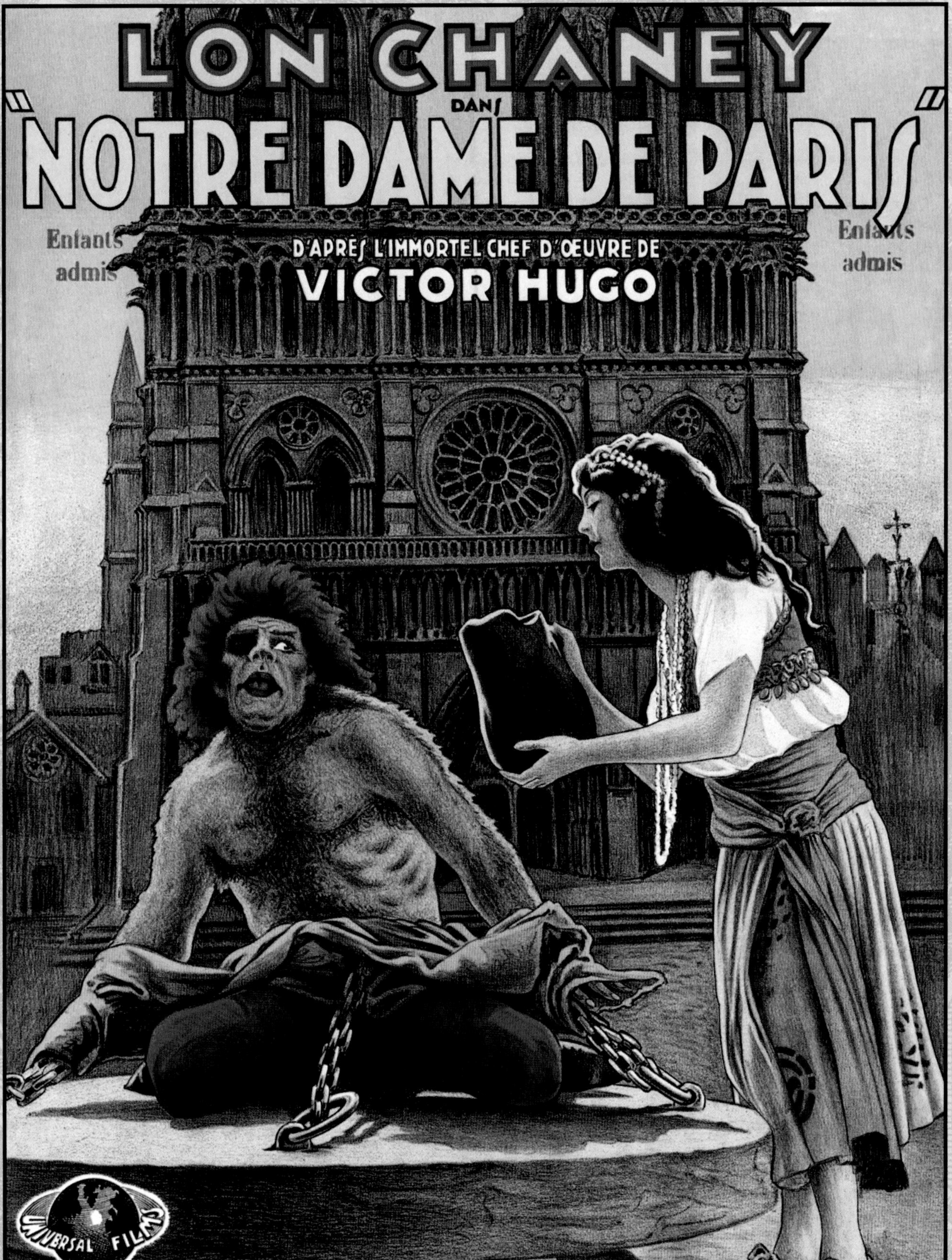
LON CHANEY
DANS
"NOTRE DAME DE PARIS"
Enfants admis
Enfants admis
D'APRÉS L'IMMORTEL CHEF D'ŒUVRE DE
VICTOR HUGO
UNIVERSAL FILMS

ABOVE: *Charles Laughton, as the Hunchback, contemplates a statue inside the cathedral in this movie still from the 1939 version of* The Hunchback of Notre Dame. **OPPOSITE:** *A still from the British film noir* Secret People, *starring Audrey Hepburn, 1952.*

ABOVE: *A wedding party at the cathedral in 1910.* **OPPOSITE:** *Karen Radkai used Notre-Dame as a backdrop for her 1955 photo of a model wearing a Jacques Griffe wedding dress in this image for* Vogue. **FOLLOWING PAGES:** *Tourists enjoying the view from the roof of the cathedral, August 1968.*

CELESTIAL ART AND MUSIC

In the 1600s, Notre-Dame began receiving an annual treasure from the goldsmiths' guild of Paris; every spring, the guild would commission a large-scale painting that it would give as a gift to the cathedral. Each painting was publically displayed at Notre-Dame—one of the first regular exhibitions of contemporary art in the city. The people had their own modern museum beneath the vaults of their cathedral.

The tradition grew out of a lovely ritual practiced by the goldsmiths since 1449. At midnight on the first of May, the month dedicated to Mary by the Church, the goldsmiths would place a tree decorated with ribbons and emblems in front of the cathedral as an offering to Mary. The tree stayed outside the western portals during the day and was brought inside after vespers for the night. After a month, the tree was placed in a cathedral chapel until May of the next year.

A few decades later the goldsmiths expanded this offering to include small paintings that were set in special places in the cathedral. In 1630, nearly two hundred years after the first offering was made, "the tradition was revolutionized when a yearly presentation of a canvas of very large dimensions (about 11 feet 2 inches [3.4 m] high by 9 feet [2.75 m] wide) was inaugurated," according to fine arts

The Notre-Dame choir rehearsing, 2009.

scholar Robert W. Berger. These gigantic paintings, commissioned every year from 1630 to 1707 and known as the Mays, brought art to the people while beautifying the cathedral. The majority of subjects were taken from the New Testament book of Acts, and in the spirit of the tree ceremony, each new painting was placed outside the central portal on the first day of May for everyone walking by to see.

All seventy-six Mays were seized during the French Revolution, and fifty eventually made their way back to the cathedral. While the majority were then stored, thirteen were put on display in the chapels of the nave. Among these were *The Conversion of St. Paul* by Laurent de la Hyre (1637), *The Crucifixion of St. Andrew* by Charles Le Brun (1647), *The Prophet Agabus Predicting to Saint Paul His Sufferings in Jerusalem* by Louis Chéron (1687), and *The Sons of Sceva Beaten by the Demon* by Mathieu Elyas (1702).

Other masterpieces of the cathedral include Jean Jouvenet's *The Visitation* (1716), which also found its way home after the revolution and was hung in the

ABOVE: *Three of the grand "Mays" paintings, from left to right,* The Descent of the Holy Spirit *by Jacques Blanchard (1634),* The Crucifiction of St. Peter *by Sébastien Bourdon (1643),* The Stoning of St. Stephen *by Charles Le Brun (1651).* **OPPOSITE:** The Visitation *by Jean Jouvenet, 1716—one of the finest paintings of the cathedral—which is normally found in the Saint-Guillaume chapel, was saved from the fire and sent to the Louvre for any necessary restoration.*

J. Jouvenet. Dextrà paralyti

Saint-Guillaume chapel. The painting depicts the story, as told in Luke, of Mary, pregnant with Jesus, visiting her cousin Elizabeth, who is pregnant with John the Baptist. Mary extends her arm toward an angel who hovers above her, and the glow of Mary's halo is brightened by the soft light coming in from the chapel's stained glass window. The visual arts of painting, sculpture, carvings, and exterior statuary reveal the lifetime of the cathedral through evolving artistic styles and periods. The music of Notre-Dame does the same.

The history of Western classical music begins with the medieval chant sung for the Latin Mass, and Notre-Dame de Paris holds a renowned place in that story. Plainchant, or Gregorian chant, has resonated in Notre-Dame since the first masses were held in the twelfth century.

Some of the first examples of polyphony, two or more independent melodies sounding at the same time as opposed to a single melody of chant, were heard at the cathedral with the music of twelfth-century French composers Léonin and Pérotin. The style of their compositions, known as the Notre Dame school, added one or more lines of melody above the chant line. The hallmark of the Notre Dame school was the ornate flight of many notes above one single, droned note of the chant (a technique called *organum*). No other style of polyphony featured such elaborate vocal writing as the Notre Dame school.

ABOVE: *Auguste Mestral's 1851 photograph shows* Virgin and Child *by sculptor Adolphe-Victor Geoffroy-Dechaume at the construction site before being lifted into place in front of the rose window above the main portal. The statue was commissioned by Viollet-le-Duc during the restoration of the cathedral.* OPPOSITE: *Eugène Atget's 1908 photo of* The Tomb of Claude d'Harcourt, *sculpted by Jean-Baptiste Pigalle in 1774, is found in the Saint-Guillaume chapel.*

Paris. 1908. (IVme Arrt.)

Eglise Notre Dame. Tombeau de Claude d'Harcourt par Pigalle

From medieval music to French Romantic music of the late eighteenth to early twentieth century, which gave us the great organ music of César Franck, Charles-Marie Widor, Maurice Duruflé, and many others, the cathedral's musical history lives side by side with its spiritual and architectural legacies.

The cathedral's organs, like its musical styles, evolved through the centuries. The first built-in organ (the earliest organs were small portable instruments) was built on the east side of the cathedral in the early fourteenth century. By the year 1400, this organ was in such poor condition that a patron gifted the cathedral a new organ to be built by organ maker Federicus Schambantz. This organ was built on the west side of the cathedral, high up in a gallery that had been used as a stage for miracle plays about the lives and feats of saints. A new organ, completed in 1403, had one manual (keyboard) and six hundred tin pipes. This same organ was restored, rebuilt, and expanded several times, and it managed to survive the French Revolution by being on hand to boom out "La Marseillaise," the majestic song written during the revolution that remains the French national anthem.

The organ was completely rebuilt by Aristide Cavaillé-Coll (1811–99) during Viollet-le-Duc's restoration of the cathedral. Cavaillé-Coll retained some of the medieval pipes, which are still in use today; added many more, for a total of nearly eight thousand; and expanded the organ to five manuals, a pedalboard, and eighty-six stops (the knobs connected to specific sets of pipes).

As in all organs of the time, air was blown through the pipes via large bellows that had to be pumped by hand. The six organ pumpers of Notre-Dame were "usually indigents recruited from the quays along the Seine," writes Rollin Smith in his biography of Louis Vierne, the principal organist at Notre-Dame from 1900 to 1937. "Vierne was at the mercy of what he humorously referred to as '*la soufflierie à alcool*'—the alcoholic wind supply!" Technology put that era to rest in 1924 when an electrical blower system went online.

Another built-in organ has its home in the choir at the east end of the cathedral, but the symphonic Cavaillé-Coll organ is not only one of the greatest treasures of

OPPOSITE: *The cathedral's Cavaillé-Coll organ is one of the most magnificent instruments in Europe. Among the great organ's approximately 8,000 pipes are a few from the original instrument built in 1403.*

"When you play the organ, the stones are singing."

—PHILIPPE LEFEBVRE, NOTRE-DAME PRINCIPAL ORGANIST

the cathedral but also one of the most magnificent instruments in Europe. Following a few modifications from 1900 to 1975, the great organ was given a complete restoration in 1992 to restore Cavaillé-Coll's symphonic sound. Today, principal organists Oliver Latry, Vincent Dubois, and Philippe Lefebvre rotate to play the great organ for masses and celebrations, and organists throughout the world are invited to perform in Saturday evening organ programs and organ recitals scheduled as part of the cathedral's concert series.

Concert organist Stephen Hamilton, who studied with French organist Marie-Claire Alain and has performed in the cathedral's Saturday evening series, describes the great organ as "one of the most colorful-sounding instruments ever conceived." He recommends listening to the organ both during a mass, to hear it "in the context in which it was designed," and at an organ concert, where you can hear all the tonal and dynamic contrasts. "Everyone says they want to hear the organ full blast, but you also want to hear it quietly and with all the gradations of color in between," he said.

The resonant acoustics of the cathedral give everything from Gregorian chants to a Bach organ prelude a unique richness that plays into the experience of performing on the great organ. "The timber forest of the roof, the plaster beneath it, and the stone walls and floor make the space a naturally vibrating entity," Hamilton said. "There is a four- or five-second reverberation, and who doesn't sound better in a vibrant room?" The French organ composers took advantage of those acoustics, he explained, and playing at the cathedral brings them to mind. "Sitting at that organ, you think of all the history in the space, like Bonaparte parading below. You think of the great organists who went before you, the masters Widor, [Olivier] Messiaen, [Marcel] Dupré, [Jean] Langlais, Duruflé, Vierne, and Jehan and Marie-Claire Alain. You realize that you are at the most historic and prestigious of the European organs."

OPPOSITE: *Notre-Dame organist Philippe Lefebvre, August 2010.*

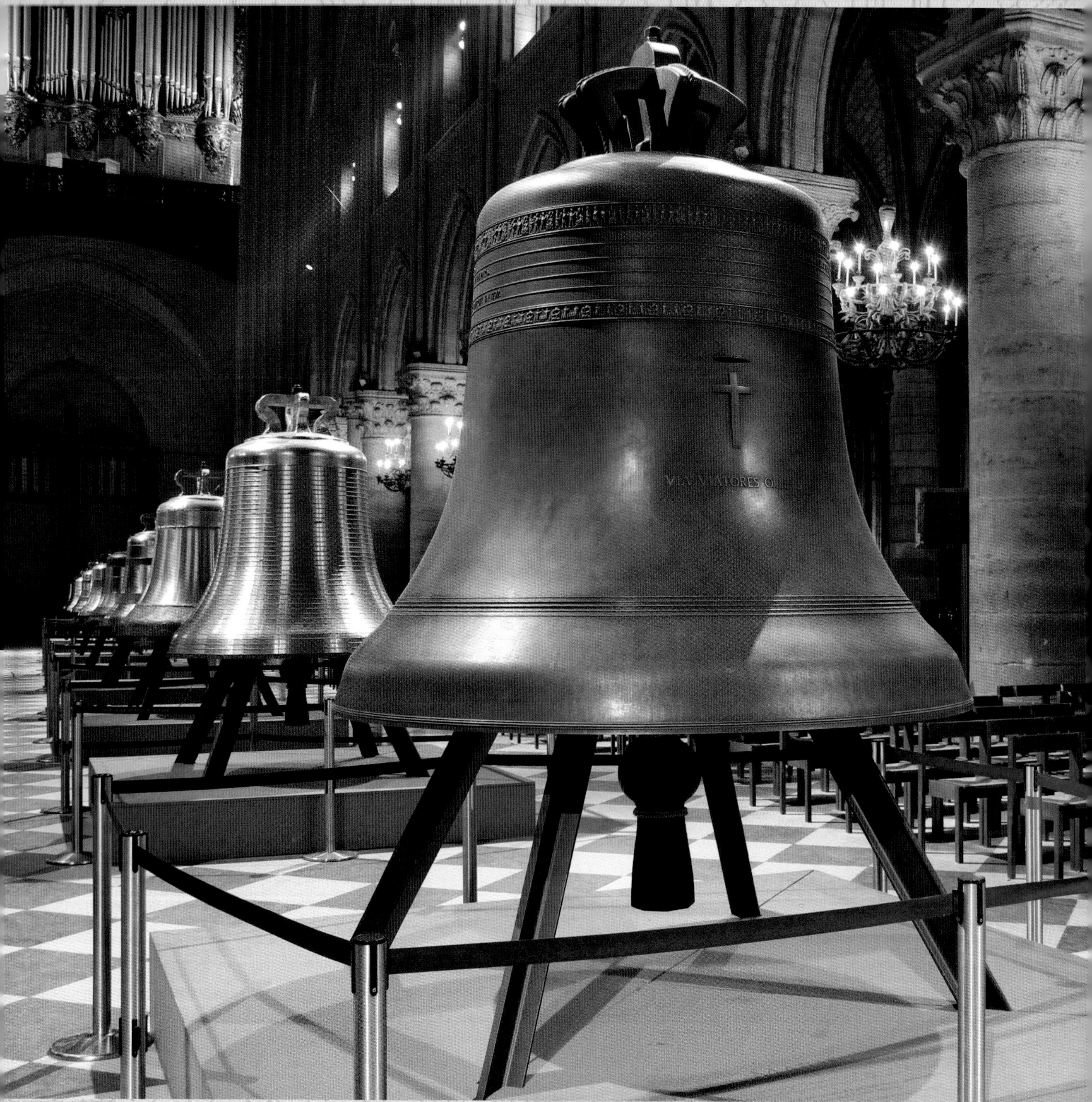
VIA VIATORES

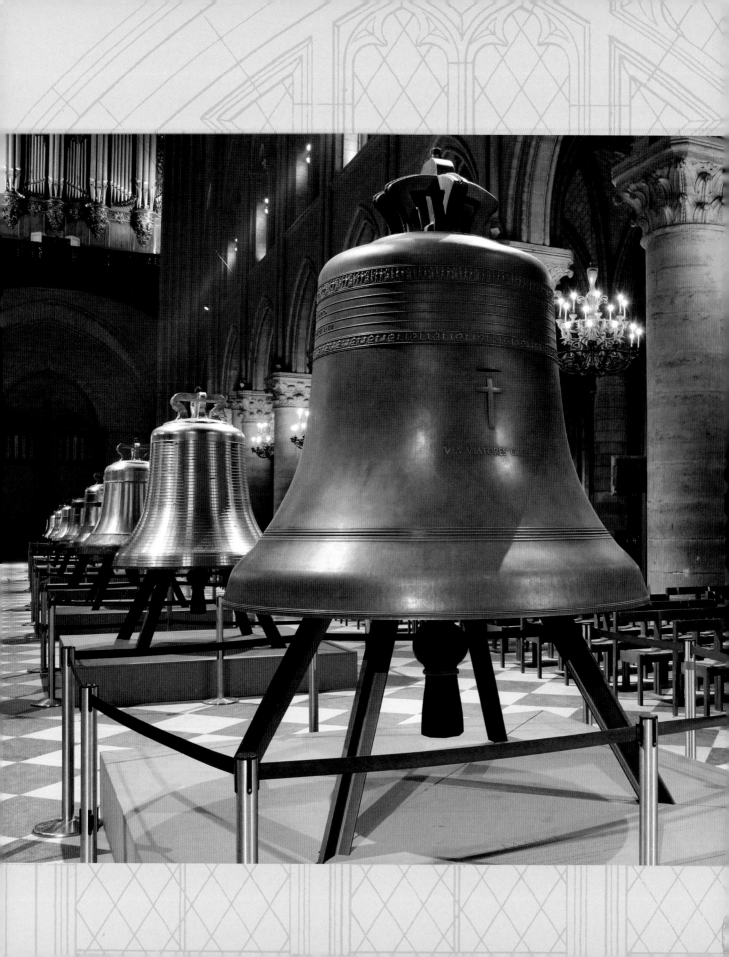

The Bells

Bells have been ringing from the towers of Notre-Dame de Paris since the late twelfth century, before construction of the cathedral was even completed.

The soundscape these bells created was silenced during the French Revolution when all but one, the thirteen-ton Emmanuel bell in the south tower, were melted down to make cannon balls. Napoleon III directed four new bells to be cast and hung in the north tower. Unfortunately, these bells were poorly tuned and not harmonious with the Emmanuel bell, and Parisians had to endure their discordant sound for more than 150 years.

Emmanuel was abandoned again in 2012 when the rest of the bells were removed to be replaced by new ones in time for the 850th anniversary of the cathedral in 2013. Eight of the nine bronze bells were cast in a foundry in Normandy that used ancient as well as modern techniques to create perfectly tuned and time-resistant bronze instruments worthy of singing with the famously resonant, deep-toned Emmanuel bell.

In February 2013, the gleaming new bells were lined up in the central aisle of the cathedral. On February 2, parish archbishop André Vingt-Trois blessed the bells during a feast-day ceremony—a blessing ritual that dates back at least 1,200 years in the Catholic Church—and the bells were left on display for the public until the end of the month. On March 23, 2013, the start of Holy Week, the newly installed bells rang for the first time. Parisians had not heard harmonious bells from the cathedral towers for at least seven generations.

The bells have not been rung by ropes since 1930, when an electrical system connected to chains took over the task. The system is now run by a computer, bringing the cathedral's towers squarely into the twenty-first century.

An exhibition in Notre-Dame's central aisle showcasing its newest bells, 2013.

ABOVE: *European bishops' procession into Notre-Dame on Good Friday, April 10, 2009.* **OPPOSITE:** *All the bishops, priests, and deacons of the Diocese of Paris, along with over 2,000 parishioners, attend the Messe Chrism as Cardinal Vingt-Trois blesses the holy chrism (myrrh), the scented oil used for sacraments, April 4, 2012.* **FOLLOWING PAGES:** *Notre-Dame at Christmas, 2007.*

ABOVE: *André Vingt-Trois, the archbishop of Paris, knocking at the main entrance door of Notre-Dame with his crozier on Palm Sunday, April 10, 2012. This ancient Catholic tradition symbolizes Jesus Christ opening God's door, the door between God and humanity.* **OPPOSITE:** *Exit procession of the Messe Chrism, March 27, 2013.*

EN FLAMMES 4

THE FIRE OF 2019

On Monday of Holy Week, April 15, 2019, as the last Mass of the evening was under way, a light lit up on the console in Notre-Dame de Paris's security control center. According to the timeline reported by France 24, the state-owned television network, the time was 6:16 p.m., and the alert signaled that smoke was detected in the Forest, the timber attic that supported the roof. Five minutes later, as security checked the Forest, the fire alarm sounded and worshippers, clergy, and staff left the building. After a short wait outside, they were given an all-clear and invited back in. The alarm sounded again at 6:30 p.m., and the evacuation proceeded for a second time. When personnel returned to the attic, they found flames at the base of the spire. The Paris Fire Brigade received the call at 6:51 p.m., and their trucks began racing through city traffic toward the Ile de la Cité.

The blaze spread throughout the wooden framework, melting the lead roof and sending a dark cloud of lead-laced smoke into the air. Hundreds of firefighters aimed their hoses toward the burning timbers from the ground and aloft in cherry pickers, while others worked

PREVIOUS PAGES: *A huge column of smoke rising above Notre-Dame as one of the world's most famous landmarks burns, April 15, 2019.* **OPPOSITE:** *Flames and smoke billow around the gargoyles and chimeras decorating the roof and sides of Notre-Dame Cathedral, April 15, 2019.*

inside to save the cathedral's priceless relics and works of art. Forming a human chain with cathedral staff and members of the Ministry of Culture, who had arrived within a half hour of news of the fire, the firefighters followed a contingency evacuation plan that prioritized objects to be removed. First came the relics stored in the sacristy, the small building connected to the south wall of the choir built by Viollet-le-Duc in the nineteenth century. "One of the first items to come out was the crown of thorns and the remnants of the crucifix," recalled an insurance adjuster assigned to assess the damage of the cathedral's treasures. "They were on the top of the list, and they were taken out in priority in strict application of the plan." More objects were whisked out of the sacristy, followed by paintings and sculptures from other locations in the cathedral.

Above the rescuers, the three-hundred-foot (91.4 m) spire, another Viollet-le-Duc addition built according to the cathedral's original plans, was engulfed in flames. At 7:51 p.m., just over an hour after the fire was discovered, throngs of Parisian onlookers and millions watching on television witnessed the spire break, collapse, and fall through the burning timbers of the roof to disappear inside. No one inside was injured when the spire crashed to the marble floor. A joystick-operated robot equipped with a water cannon was brought in to fight the flames from the most dangerous angles inside the cathedral.

As an orange glow lit up the evening sky above the cathedral, twenty firefighters climbed the towers with their gear and hoses, risking their lives to fight the fire from the inside and create a wall of water to protect the wooden belfries of the towers. Fire had already reached the north tower, and if the towers fell, the entire cathedral could collapse. Saving the north tower meant saving the south tower—and the entire cathedral. In fifteen decisive minutes, the firefighters dowsed the flames in the north tower and won the greatest battle of the night. Firefighters continued drowning the last flames and embers for another ten hours, finishing their nearly fifteen-hour battle as the city went back to work on Tuesday morning.

The fire brigade suspected that the fire was caused by an electrical short in equipment being used for the $6.8 million restoration project that had begun in 2018. Weather and pollution were eroding and weakening the flying buttresses,

OPPOSITE: *Notre-Dame can be seen on fire over the rooftops of Paris.*

crumbling gargoyles had been replaced with plastic pipe, broken stone railings were patched together with wood, chips and blocks of limestone were falling off the walls, and cracks appearing in the stone warned of potential instability. At the time of the fire, the cathedral was covered in scaffolding for the restoration.

Much was saved, but some was lost. The rooster that sat atop the spire was found dented but intact, although the status of the three relics the rooster contained—including a thorn from the cathedral's most prized relic, the crown of thorns purported to be worn by Jesus at his crucifixion—was not yet reported by June 2019. The crown of thorns itself was saved, as well as a section of wood that Catholics believe to be from the crucifixion cross, the robe of Saint Louis, and other relics and treasures stored in the sacristy. The Mays paintings that had graced the walls of the cathedral for more than four hundred years and Jean Jouvenet's *The Visitation* also survived and were sent to the Louvre for safekeeping with the rest of the art. Another treasure, the fourteenth-century statue of Mary holding the baby Jesus that stood on a pillar at the transept, was rescued without harm. Known as *Notre-Dame de Paris*, this life-size statue is the most well known of the

"I join in your sadness . . . for Notre-Dame . . . [the] architectural and spiritual heritage of Paris, France, and humanity."

—Pope Francis II

thirty-seven statutes of Mary in the cathedral and depicts Mary in a crown with Jesus tugging at a fold of her robe.

Astonishingly, the cathedral's three rose windows remained intact during the inferno, whose temperatures reached up to 1,700 degrees Fahrenheit (927°C). The survival of these thirteenth-century masterpieces was "a bit of a miracle," said André Finot, the cathedral's spokesman. The great organ, situated beneath the stone roof at the west end of the cathedral, was also spared. The main altar of the choir and the gold cross standing behind it survived, creating an inspirational image when the first pictures of the interior were reported after the fire. The 1725 pietà in white marble by Nicolas Coustou (1658–1733) also escaped damage at the main altar, as did the statues of Louis XIV (c. 1708, by Antoine Coysevox) and Louis XIII (1715, by Guillaume Coustou, Nicolas's brother) that kneel at each side of it. Seventy-eight ornately carved wooden choir stalls, built in the eighteenth century and set in two facing rows, were also unscathed.

In another fortunate twist, the copper statues of the apostles and four evangelists on the roof that surrounded the base of the spire had been removed with a crane and loaded onto trucks just four days before the fire. By Holy Monday, they were safely awaiting restoration at a facility in southwestern France.

The majority of the cathedral's art was saved, but the 5 to 10 percent that was lost cannot be replaced. Other losses, however, can be restored. The choir organ, damaged by water and heat, can be repaired; the incinerated attic, spire, lead roof, and stone vault section can be replaced; and the day after the fire, President Emmanuel Macron vowed that they would be.

OPPOSITE: *A Parisian captures the catastrophe on his cell phone, April 15, 2019.*
FOLLOWING PAGES: *Notre-Dame, roofless.*

28 30
32

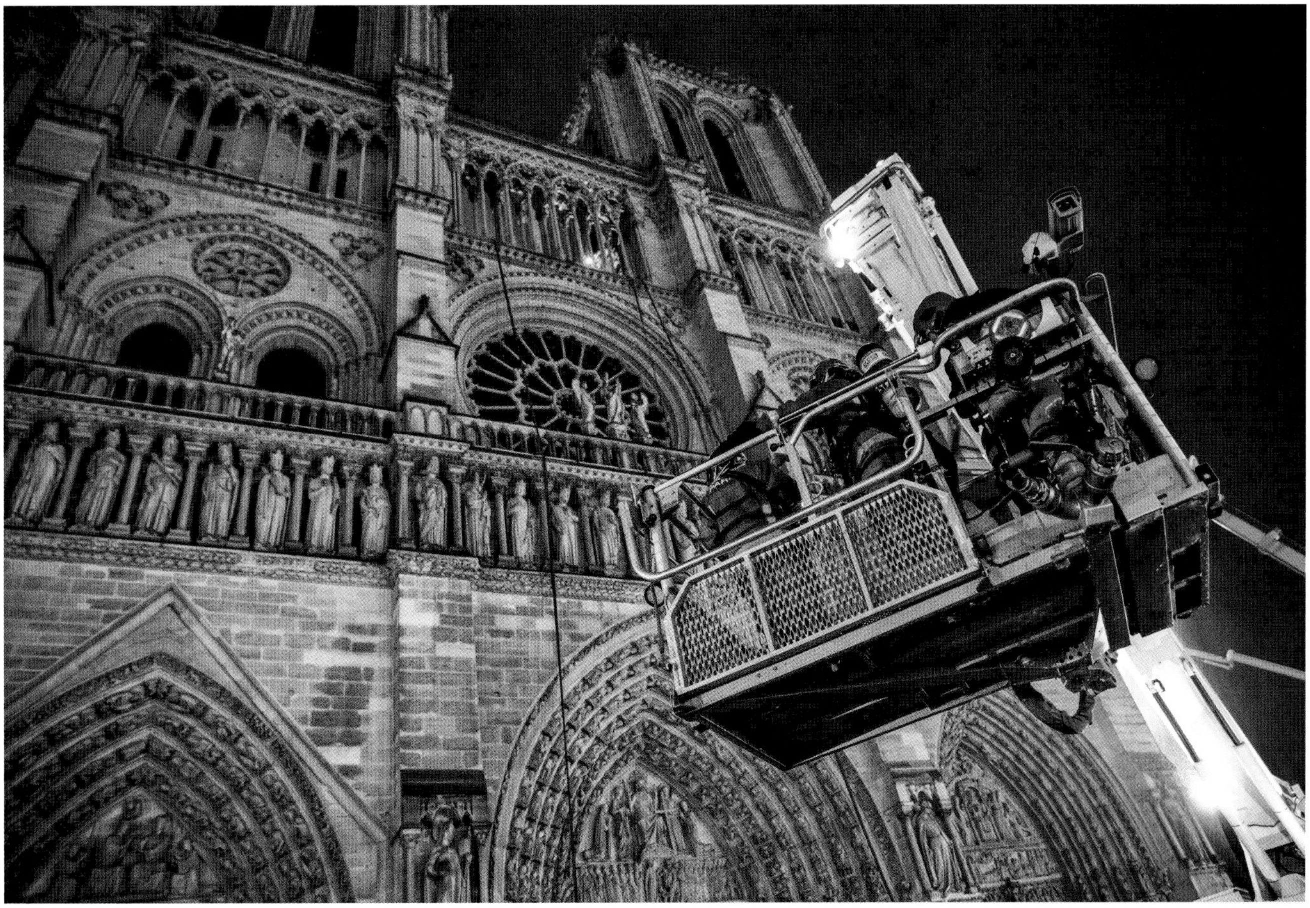

"Dear General Gallet, at the peril of your life you have saved part of our own lives."

—ANNE HIDALGO, MAYOR OF PARIS, TO FIRE BRIGADE COMMANDER JEAN-CLAUDE GALLET

PREVIOUS PAGES: *People gather along the Seine to watch in shock as the fire engulfs Notre-Dame.* OPPOSITE: *The April 15, 2019, fire seen through the upper south window, with the roof completely gone.* ABOVE: *Firefighters spray water onto Notre-Dame Cathedral during a visit by French president Emmanuel Macron, April 15, 2019.*

ABOVE: *An interior view of the cathedral one day after the devastating fire of 2019.*
OPPOSITE: *A crowd in front of Notre-Dame Cathedral assessing the damage, April 17, 2019.*

Saving Treasures and Holy Relics

Notre-Dame de Paris holds treasures known as its "very own crown jewels," a collection of priceless objects gathered through the ages. Held in the sacristy built by Viollet-le-Duc in the mid-1800s, they include gold- and gemstone-encrusted chalices, crucifixes, procession crosses, bishops' rings and miters, candelabras, and illuminated liturgical books. More precious than these to the archdiocese, however, is the cathedral's collection of holy relics: the crown of thorns, a fragment of the wooden cross, and a nail from the cross.

One of these receives special attention on particular days of the year, including Fridays during Lent. On Friday, March 29, 2019, for example, less than three weeks before fire erupted in Notre-Dame de Paris, a solemn procession advanced toward the high altar of the cathedral. Men and women from the Order of the Holy Sepulchre, the organization that protects the cathedral's holy relics, walked in silence behind the priest who carried a crystal and gold container on a red velvet cushion. The tube-shaped reliquary contained the crown of thorns (opposite), described as "one of the holiest relics of Christendom, second only to the Shroud of Turin." After reaching the altar, the priest turned and presented the relic to the people kneeling at their pews. After a brief homily, each parishioner was invited to walk up and venerate the relic with a touch or a kiss.

This ceremony takes place in the cathedral every first Friday of the month as well as every Friday during Lent. The crown of thorns (opposite), believed by Catholics to have been placed on Jesus's head before his crucifixion, is one of three relics brought to Paris in 1239 by King Louis IX (1214–70), who had purchased them from Emperor Baldwin II of Constantinople. The circle of braided rushes originally held seventy thorns, which French kings gave away as gifts over the centuries.

Louis IX's relics also included a piece of wood believed to be from the cross on which Jesus was crucified. The fragment, about nine inches (23 cm) long, is also kept in a crystal case in the treasury. The third famous relic from this group is a nail considered to be a remnant of the cross. To house the relics, the king built the stunning Sainte-Chapelle (Holy Chapel) in the courtyard of the royal palace on the Île de la Cité. After Napoleon restored the Catholic Church in 1801, the relics were moved to Notre-Dame de Paris. Another relic stored in the cathedral's treasury related to the crown of thorns, fragment of the cross, and nail is the tunic worn by King Louis IX as he brought the relics to Paris. The king was canonized as Saint Louis in 1297.

Each of these relics was rescued during the fire of April 15, 2019, along with other treasures that had been stored in the sacristy.

OPPOSITE: *Before the fire broke out, the sixteen nineteenth-century copper statues that normally grace the base of the spire—the twelve apostles and four evangelists—had already been safely stored at the SOCRA workshop in Marsac-sur-l'Isle near Bordeaux, awaiting restoration. Shown here, the statue of Saint Matthew the evangelist, symbolized as the winged man.* **ABOVE:** *Rubble strewn in front of Nicolas Coustou's pietà and cross, at the altar inside Notre-Dame, May 15, 2019.*

Our History Never Ends

Address by President Emmanuel Macron, Élysée Palace, April 16, 2019

My dear compatriots, the fire of Notre-Dame de Paris has deeply touched the hearts and minds of Parisians, the French people, and the entire world.

Tonight we entered this cathedral, which belongs to an entire nation and its millennial history. The fire had just been vanquished. The firefighters had stopped the fire by taking the most extreme risks and were there, around us, with their leaders, viewing the devastated roofs. They were twenty or twenty-five years old and from all parts of France, from all backgrounds, but what we saw that night together in Paris is this ability to mobilize, to unite in order to conquer. In the course of our history, we have built cities, ports, churches. Many have burned or been destroyed by wars, revolutions, or the faults of men. Every time, every time, we rebuilt them.

The Notre-Dame fire reminds us that our history never ends, never, and that we will always have challenges to overcome, and that what we believe to be indestructible can also reach its limit. All that makes France material and spiritual is alive and for that very reason is fragile, and we must not forget it. And again it is up to the French of today to ensure over time the great continuity that makes the French nation, and for that reason tonight I wanted to address you directly because this is our duty today, the one that we must have in mind, nothing less.

> **"We will rebuild Notre-Dame cathedral even more beautifully."**

I will come back to you as I promised in the coming days so that we can act collectively to resolve our great debate, but today is not the time for that. Tomorrow politics and its tumult will regain their place, as we all know, but that moment has not yet come. Let us now remember the last hours. Last night, tonight, this morning, everyone gave what they had. The firefighters fought heroically, risking their lives. The police, the emergency workers were there, as always. Parisians have been comforting each other. The French trembled, deeply moved. Foreigners cried. The journalists wrote, the writers dreamed, the photographers showed the world these terrible images. Rich and poor alike gave money. Everyone has given what they can, everyone in their place, everyone in their role, and this evening I tell you this: we are truly a nation of builders. We have so much to rebuild. So yes, we will rebuild Notre-Dame cathedral even more beautifully, and I want it to be completed within five years. We can, and we will organize ourselves. After this time of trial will come a time of reflection, then a time of action, but let us not confuse them. Let us not fall into the trap of acting in haste.

I understand, like you; I know all the pressures. I know, in a way, the kind of false impatience that would make it necessary to react at every moment, to announce plans for certain dates as if being the head of a country was only about administering things and not being aware of our history, of the times of women and men. I believe very deeply that it is up to us to transform this catastrophe into a moment to become—while reflecting deeply on what we have been, and what we should be—better than what we are. It is up to us to find the thread of our national project, the one that made us, that unites us, a human project, passionately French. Ladies, gentlemen, and all of you who love France and love Paris, I want to tell you tonight that I share your pain, but I also share your hope. We must now get to work. We will act and we will succeed. Long live the Republic and long live France.

ABOVE: *French president Emmanuel Macron at the Élysée Palace paying tribute to the firefighters and security forces who helped save Notre-Dame from complete destruction, April 18, 2019.*

We Will Rebuild

Three hours after the blaze began, President Macron addressed the traumatized nation from the steps of the cathedral, describing Notre-Dame as France's "history, our literature, the epicenter of our life, the cathedral of every French person," and promising to rebuild it. The next day, he canceled his much-anticipated speech about the ongoing protests of the *gilets jaunes* (yellow vests/jackets) movement that had rocked the country for months in opposition to a proposed gas tax increase and Macron's policies in general. (The movement's name came from the neon vests French drivers wear in case of an emergency.) Instead, the president gave a televised speech about the fire, declaring that the country would build the cathedral to be more beautiful than it was and complete the project in five years.

Live television broadcasts of the fire had impacted the world like a seismic shock, uniting people in grief and despair. A video of Parisians singing "Ave Maria" as they watched the fire from a street went viral on Twitter and had more than twelve million views. World leaders expressed their condolences and solidarity, including Pope Francis II in letter to Paris archbishop Michel Aupetit and the people of France,

Temporary tarpaulins cover the roof of Notre-Dame to protect it from rain damage, June 13, 2019.

in which he recognized Notre-Dame de Paris as a testimony to the Catholic faith as well as a "national symbol dear to the hearts of Parisians and French people, in the diversity of their convictions." Former First Lady Michelle Obama posted a photo of herself with Barack and their young daughters Malia and Sasha on a visit to Notre-Dame and shared the dramatic impression the cathedral had made when she first visited it on a school trip. "The feeling was almost indescribable—a place that lifts you to a higher understanding of who we are and who we can be," she wrote on Instagram.

Pledges of financial support poured in at the same time, starting with notices from three of France's wealthiest citizens. "Faced with this tragedy, my father and I have decided to contribute to the funds needed to fully rebuild Notre Dame de Paris, in order to bring this jewel of our heritage back to life as soon as possible," tweeted François-Henri Pinault, CEO of Kering (owners of Gucci, Yves Saint Laurent, and other brands). Bernard Jean Étienne Arnault, chairman of LMVH, the largest group of luxury brands in the world, tweeted that his family and company would donate €200 million ($224 million) to the cathedral's reconstruction. Also in those first hours, French cosmetics company L'Oréal pledged 100 million euros ($112 million), as did Patrick Pouyanné, CEO of Total, the French energy company.

While awaiting the nearly $1 billion in promised donations from France's wealthiest families and companies, the cathedral relied on foundations and small donations to pay the salaries of its approximately 150 out-of-work employees. In particular, the Friends of Notre-Dame de Paris foundation, founded by Michel Picaud in 2017, provided much of these funds, and Picaud estimated that 90 percent of its donors were Americans. His foundation had launched the restoration project already under way at the cathedral and was now meeting the first needs of those most impacted by the loss.

The cathedral's music managed to stay alive during Holy Week, thanks to an invitation from Saint-Sulpice, the largest church in Paris. For the first time in centuries, Notre-Dame de Paris's choirs sang outside its walls during Holy Week when it sang for Saint-Sulpice's evening Mass on Holy Thursday. More than two thousand attended the Mass that welcomed Notre-Dame's "refugee" choirs, including one with singers ages nine to eighteen. After this youthful and obviously emotional group sang, the parishioners could not help but give them a standing ovation.

A month after the fire, the public and political debates about restoration took on a new sense of urgency. An engineering analysis revealed that the cathedral had lost more than half of its wind resistance. Without every element of the unitary system that stabilized the building, the structure would not likely withstand winds higher than fifty-five miles (89 km/h) per hour. Workers had recently placed temporary covers over the empty sections of the roof to protect the interior and hollow sections of the remaining vaults from rain, but engineer Paolo Vannucci's report alerted restorers about the urgent need for reinforcements. The new fragility of the cathedral, according to Vannucci's simulations, would allow it to bear less than half of the wind speed it could withstand before the fire.

ABOVE: Choirmaster Sylvain Dieudonné conducting the Ensemble vocal de Notre-Dame de Paris in Saint-Sulpice church, three days after fire devastated Notre-Dame.

A Stable Balance of Forces

Could a video game help rebuild?

After the Notre-Dame de Paris fire of April 15, 2019, the Italian design and architecture magazine *designboom* suggested a video game as a potential tool for the reconstruction. Ubisoft's *Assassin's Creed® Unity*, an action-adventure video game set in Paris during the French Revolution, features a three-dimensional cathedral (opposite) created in painstaking detail (with a few creative innovations) by digital artist Caroline Miousse. Assisted by a historian, Miousse spent two years recreating the cathedral in the digital studio based on images they studied. "Although it may not trump traditional architectural planning . . . the detailed measurements, material references, and close-to-exact representation make it a very detailed and reliable resource," claimed the *designboom* writers.

While Miousse's digital cathedral is undoubtedly capturing new fans of Notre-Dame de Paris, reconstruction workers will more likely look to art historian Andrew Tallon's (1969–2018) 3-D rendering of the cathedral, meticulously drawn from laser scans placed in more than fifty locations inside and outside the building. Tallon's 2015 digital model, accurate to within five millimeters, is composed of a billion points of data that create a hauntingly beautiful "point cloud" image of Notre-Dame. In turn, the digital model reveals answers about the cathedral's construction that have been debated for decades, such as the timing of the addition of the flying buttresses.

Some historians have argued that the buttresses, while among the earliest built in French Gothic style, were not part of the original design. Tallon's rendering, however, proves that they were there from the beginning. The stone vaults, a collection of pointed arches, should push the walls outward, but Tallon found that "the upper part of the building has not moved one smidgen in eight hundred years." This means the flying buttresses were there from the beginning, "pushing the walls inward and creating a stable balance of forces," Tallon said.

The exquisite accuracy of Tallon's model also revealed a discovery about the western wall and facade. His laser scans showed that the line of statues called the Gallery of Kings that sweeps across the facade above the portals is out of plumb by almost one foot. Tallon interpreted this startling measurement as evidence that the unstable soil beneath the facade caused the structure to lean forward and to the north. Construction must have stopped until the ground had compressed enough for work to resume—approximately ten years!

This news entered the mix of concerns about the government's role in paying for reconstruction (while the state owns the cathedral, the diocese is responsible for its upkeep), the feasibility of the president's ambitious five-year goal—which would complete the reconstruction in time for the 2024 Paris Summer Olympics—and what sort of design philosophy would be used. In terms of design, the big question discussed throughout France was: Should Paris follow Viollet-le-Duc's principle of respecting each style that made its way into the structure through the centuries or instead make a modern statement?

Paris mayor Anne Hidalgo announced her preference for a restoration identical to the cathedral as it stood prior to the fire. Other traditionalists felt the same. However, days after the fire, French prime minister Édouard Philippe launched an international design competition for rebuilding the roof-spire combination, asking designers to imagine a fresh look "adapted to the techniques and the challenges of our era." First entries included a crystal glass roof that swept up into a spire to create a unified canopy with gardens beneath. Another envisioned a greenhouse roof design with a spire for housing beehives, a gesture to honor the famed beehives living above the cathedral sacristy, which survived the fire. One submission

imagined the roof as a covered park, "a sanctuary for animals and insects even more threatened in cities," with a spire that emitted a beam of white light toward the heavens. Another designer proposed replacing the roof and vaults with stained glass, which would allow colored light to stream into the cathedral during the day and be backlit for a stunning exterior view at night. In this design, the spire would also be a swirling column of stained glass.

What will Paris decide? By the time of this writing in June 2019, decisions on design, funding, and timing were still in process. The traditionalist design view will likely win, with the Senate and National Assembly negotiating a bill in May to restore the cathedral to "its last known visual state." Whatever the future holds for Notre-Dame de Paris, the world is with her.

OPPOSITE: *Ulf Mejergren Architects' idea for a public pool on Notre-Dame's roof. "We think that the cathedral looks much better without both the spire and the lead-clad roof. Instead we let the bell towers, the flying buttresses, and the rose windows do the talking."* **ABOVE:** *Parisian architectural firm Studio NAB wants to integrate apiaries into a gold-toned steel-and-glass spire to produce "nectar of the gods" and create a greenhouse where the Forest (the burned oak framework) is reused to create planters watched over by the apostles Viollet-le-Duc created.*

ABOVE: *POA Estudio in Córdoba, Spain, envisions a new spire made of eight glass panels that reflect the light and project it inside. Inspired by the iconic Gothic stained glass windows of the cathedral, the space would open to the heavens, breathe, and transform with the surroundings.* **OPPOSITE:** *Eight Inc., the original Apple store architects, is interested in respecting the design, scale, and texture of the original building while expressing "the soul's longing for God," and envisions replicating the old roof and spire entirely in glass.*

"The firefighters . . . did a remarkable job. . . . The cathedral is the fruit of human genius; it is the masterpiece of man. The human being is the fruit of divine genius; it is the masterpiece of God. . . . The profound reason why Notre-Dame cathedral was built [was] to manifest man's inner impulse toward God."

—Michel Aupetit, archbishop of Paris

RIGHT: *Michel Aupetit, the archbishop of Paris, in a side chapel of Notre-Dame, leading the first Mass at the cathedral since the April fire, Saturday, June 15, 2019.*
FOLLOWING PAGES: *A night view across the Seine toward Notre-Dame, May 1, 1988.*

"She will remain standing, again and again, defying the times."

—General Jean-Louis Georgelin, director of Notre-Dame de Paris restoration

ACKNOWLEDGMENTS

Sterling Publishing is extremely grateful to book producer Esther Margolis of Newmarket Publishing Management Corporation, who, as always, skillfully and miraculously worked with us to produce a very special book on a very short schedule. We are also grateful to Antonia Felix for writing such a meaningful text that was at once comprehensive and concise. Special thanks as always to the outstanding photo editor, researcher, and caption writer Christopher Measom and his partner, Timothy Shaner, designer extraordinaire, at Night & Day Design, who yet again made the impossible possible. We thank all of them for their dedication and expertise.

Antonia Felix expresses thanks to Esther Margolis for making this project happen and for steering us all into motion. She is grateful to Stephen Hamilton for his interview and expertise on Notre-Dame de Paris's great organ and to Julie Conrad for her generous assistance with translation. Thanks and admiration to Barbara Berger, executive editor at Sterling, for her meticulous editing and guidance. Special thanks to the ever higher creative standards of Timothy Shaner and Christopher Measom, who always manage to make each of their books even more stunning than the last.

As book packager of this unique volume, Esther Margolis and Newmarket wish to acknowledge and thank the following for their over-the-top dedication and commitment to making the best book possible, deadlines permitting: the extraordinary, talented, and ever-patient designer Timothy Shaner and photo editor Christopher Measom; expert and accomplished writer Antonia Felix; and skilled social media sleuth Marie Mayhew. Special acknowledgments go to the excellent team at Sterling Publishing, including: Christine Heun, art director, interiors; David Ter-Avanesyan, cover designer; Elizabeth Lindy, senior art director, covers; Linda Liang, photography editor; Christopher Bain, photography director; Ellen Hudson, production manager; Michael Cea, production editor and indexer; and especially Barbara Berger, executive editor, whose enthusiasm and expert guidance were essential in bringing this thrilling book to life.

NOTES

INTRODUCTION

x **"Gothic architecture . . . aimed":** Jean Bony, *French Gothic Architecture of the 12th and 13th Centuries* (Berkeley: University of California Press, 1983), 61. **"eighty kings":** "Notre Dame Cathedral kicks off 850th Birthday," *Washington Examiner*, December 12, 2012.

PART I: MEDIEVAL MASTERPIECE

8 **"There is no more striking":** Allan Temko, *Notre-Dame of Paris* (New York: Viking, 1955), 103.

11 **"The human race":** Victor Hugo, *Notre-Dame de Paris* (1831; New York: Collier, 1917), 188.

12 **"I wish to honor":** Auguste Rodin, *Cathedrals of France*, trans. Elisabeth Chase Geissbuhler (1914; repr. Boston: Beacon Press, 1965), 26.

16 **"Author Victor Hugo on Gothic":** Hugo, *Notre-Dame de Paris*, 184–86. **"The transept belfry":** Ibid.,155.

23 **"The knowledge of this":** Otto von Simpson, *The Gothic Cathedral: Origins of Gothic Architecture and the Medieval Concept of Order* (Princeton, NJ: Princeton University Press, 1956), 14. **"according to true measure":** Ibid., 16.

24 **"The dominant ratios":** Nelly Shafik Ramzy, "The Dual Language of Geometry in Gothic Architecture: The Symbolic Message of Euclidian Geometry versus the Visual Dialogue of Fractal Geometry," *Peregrinations: Journal of Medieval Art and Architecture* 5, no. 5 (2015), 165.

28 **"If the Gothic architect":** Otto von Simpson, "The Gothic Cathedral: Design and Meaning," *Journal of the Society of Architectural Historians* 11, no. 3 (1952), 13.

30 **"A medieval church was not":** Alice Mary Hilton, "How to Read the Great Cathedrals of Europe," *New York Times*, April 19, 1981.

34 **"The Middle Ages loved":** Richard and Clara Winston, *Notre-Dame de Paris* (New York: Newsweek, 1971), 75.

37 **"The rose is beauty":** Temko, *Notre-Dame of Paris*, 175. **"The offer of more light":** Ibid., 239.

38 **"inexhaustible richness":** Laurent Thurnherr, "Le Chevallier of Notre-Dame," https://www.notredamedeparis.fr/en/la-cathedrale/histoire/grandes-figures-et-personnalites/jacques-le-chevallier/.

PART II: WITNESS TO HISTORY

46 **"Churches were sacked":** Carlos M. N. Eire, *War Against the Idols: The Reformation of Worship from Erasmus to Calvin* (Cambridge, UK: Cambridge University Press, 1986), 2. **"had escaped":** Alistair Horne, *Seven Ages of Paris* (New York: Knopf, 2003), 162.

47 **"Deism rather than atheism":** Charles Lyttle, "Deistic Piety in the Cults of the French Revolution," *Church History* 2, no. 1 (1933), 26.

49 **"The French people recognize":** Temko, *Notre-Dame of Paris*, 1955), 304. **"did not create kings":** Maximilien de Robespierre, Speech for the Festival of the Supreme Being, http://www.emersonkent.com/speeches/festival_of_the_supreme_being.htm. **"as the majority":** Frank J. Coppa, *Controversial Concordants: The Vatican's Relations with Napoleon, Mussolini, and Hitler* (Washington, DC: The Catholic University of America Press, 1999), 36. **"one of the chief means":** Ibid. **"cannot exist":** Ibid.

51 **"The church of Notre-Dame":** Adolphe Thiers, *History of the Consulate and the Empire of France Under Napoleon*, vol. 1, trans. D. Forbes Campbell and H. W. Herbert (Philadelphia: Carey and Hart, 1847), 636. **"that venerable pile":** "Napoleon Is Crowned Emperor," Napoleon Bonaparte, http://emperornapoleon.com/napoleon/coronation.html.

55 **"The book has lost none":** Jean-Marc Hovasse, "Introduction" in Victor Hugo, *The Hunchback of Notre-Dame* (New York: Knopf, 2012), xviii.

57 **"a focal point":** Daniel D. Reiff, "Viollet le Duc and Historic Restoration: The West Portals of Notre-Dame," *Journal of the Society of Architectural Historians* 30, no. 1 (1971), 28.

71 **"enormous sculpted beasts":** Michael Camille, *The Gargoyles of Notre-Dame: Medievalism and the Monsters of Modernity* (Chicago: University of Chicago Press, 2009), 10.

72 **"to emit cold water":** Charles de Kay, "Gargoyles Old and New," *Architectural Record* 19, no. 6 (1906), 423.

75 **"The brilliant ceremony":** "Mary & Francis' Wedding," Scotland's Mary, https://scotlandsmary.com/the-dauphin/mary-queen-of-scots-and-francois-wedding-ceremony-and-festivities/

79 **"a garment white":** Ibid.

81 **"Even his enemies":** Jeremy A. Crang, "General De Gaulle Under Sniper Fire in Notre Dame Cathedral, 26 August 1944: Robert Reid's BBC Commentary," *Historical Journal of Film, Radio and Television* 27, no. 3 (2007), 393.

83 **"Quite recently":** C. K. Austin, "Paris in Wartime," *Medical Record* 86 (1914), 1016.

83–84 **"Paris is to be transformed . . . line of fire":** Alex Kershaw, *Avenue of Spies: A True Story of Terror, Espionage, and One American Family's Heroic Resistance in Nazi-Occupied Paris* (New York: Broadway Books, 2015), 166.

84 **"a popular carnival":** Jean Edward Smith, *The Liberation of Paris: How Eisenhower, de Gaulle, and von Choltitz Saved the City of Light* (New York: Simon & Schuster, 2019), 186. **"The air crackled":** "The Liberation of Paris, 1944," EyeWitness to History, 2008, www.eyewitnesstohistory.com.

PART III: THE PEOPLE'S CATHEDRAL

96 **"Medieval people knew":** Robert Barron, *Heaven in Stone and Glass: Experiencing the Spirituality of the Great Cathedrals* (New York: Crossroad, 2000), 17. **"moves, breathes, aspires":** Temko, *Notre-Dame of Paris*, 4. **"The cathedral has incarnated":** Evelyne Cohen, "Visiter Notre-Dame de Paris," trans. Antonia Felix, *Ethnologie Français* 32, no. 3 (2002), 511.

107 **"There are no tourists":** Catholic News Agency, "Paris Archbishop at Mass: Notre-Dame Exists to be a Place of Worship," *National Catholic Register*, June 18, 2019, http://www.ncregister.com/daily-news/paris-archbishop-at-mass-notre-dame-exists-to-be-a-place-of-worship.

119 **"the tradition":** Robert W. Berger, *Public Access to Art in Paris: A Documentary History from the Middle Ages to 1800* (University Park: Pennsylvania State University Press, 1999), 54.

124 **"usually indigents . . . wind supply":** Rollin Smith, *Louis Vierne: Organist of Notre-Dame Cathedral* (Hillsdale, NY: Pendragon Press, 1999), 34.

127 **"When you play":** Alex Marshall, "Notre-Dame Musicians Rejoice That Cathedral's Organ Was Spared," *New York Times*, April 24, 2019. **"one of the most colorful . . . European organs":** Stephen Hamilton, interview with the author, May 31, 2019.

PART IV: EN FLAMMES

140 **"One of the first items":** Noor Zainab Hussain, "Insurance Adjuster Reports 90% of Notre Dame Cathedral Treasure Saved from Fire," *Insurance Journal*, April 17, 2019.

143 **"I join in your sadness":** Devin Watkins, "Notre Dame Fire: Pope Joins Paris in Sorrow, Vatican Offers Technical Expertise," *Vatican News*, April 16, 2019, https://www.vaticannews.va/en/pope/news/2019-04/pope-francis-message-notre-dame-cathedral.html. **"a bit of a miracle":** "'It's a Bit of a Miracle': Delight as Notre Dame's Iconic Rose Windows Survive Blaze," RT, April 16, 2019, https://www.rt.com/news/456714-notre-dame-rose-windows-fire/

149 **"Dear General Gallet":** "Paris Mayor Anne Hidalgo Speaks During Ceremony in Honour of Fire-fighters that Saved Notre-Dame from a Devastating Fire," France 24, April 18, 2019, https://www.france24.com/en/video/20190418-peril-life-you-have-saved-part-own-lives-says-mayor-hidalgo

152 **"very own":** "Notre-Dame de Paris Cathedral," France.fr, 2018, https://us.france.fr/en/paris/article/notre-dame-paris-cathedral. **"one of the holiest":** Jean Smits, "Jesus' Crown of Thorns Venerated During Lent by Faithful in Paris," LifeSiteNews, April 4, 2019, https://www.lifesitenews.com/blogs/crown-of-thorns-brings-the-faithful-to-their-knees-in-reverence.

159 **"history, our literature":** Jon Henley, "Macron's Gilets Jaunes Speech Is Pivotal after Notre Dame Disaster," *Guardian*, April 17, 2019.

160 **"national symbol dear to the hearts":** Philip Pullella, "Pope Shares Sadness of French over Notre Dame, Hopes for Restoration," Reuters, April 16, 2019, https://www.reuters.com/article/us-france-notredame-pope/pope-shares-sadness-of-french-over-notre-dame-hopes-for-restoration-idUSKCN1RS0TE. **"The feeling":** Guy Davies, "World Leaders React to the Notre Dame Cathedral Fire: 'My heart aches,'" ABC News, April 16, 2019, https://abcnews.go.com/International/world-leaders-react-notre-dame-cathedral-fire-part/story?id=62426332. **"Faced with this":** Nelson Oliveira, "French Billionaires Pledge More Than $600 Million to Rebuild Notre Dame Cathedral," MSN News, April 16, 2019, https://www.msn.com/en-us/news/world/french-billionaires-pledge-more-than-24600-million-to-rebuild-notre-dame-cathedral/ar-BBW03Qo.

162 **"Although it may not trump":** Kieron Marchese, "How a Video Game Could Help Rebuild the Notre Dame Cathedral, *Designboom*, April 17, 2019, https://www.designboom.com/architecture/how-a-video-game-could-help-to-rebuild-the-notre-dame-cathedral-04-17-2019/. **"upper part":** Rachel Hartigan Shea, "Historian Uses Lasers to Unlock Mysteries of Gothic Cathedrals," *National Geographic*, April 16, 2019, https://news.nationalgeographic.com/2015/06/150622-andrew-tallon-notre-dame-cathedral-laser-scan-art-history-medieval-gothic/.

164 **"adapted to the techniques":** Giedrė Vaičiulaitytė, "17 Artists Suggest Notre Dame Cathedral Reconstruction Designs," n.d., https://www.boredpanda.com/notre-dame-cathedral-new-spire-designs/?utm_source=google&utm_medium=organic&utm_campaign=organic.

165 **"a sanctuary":** Ibid. **"its last known":** Gabrielle Sorto, "France Says Notre Dame Must Be Restored Exactly the Way It Was," CNN, May 29, 2019, https://www.cnn.com/style/article/french-senate-notre-dame-restoration-scli-trnd/index.html. **"We think that the cathedral":** Andrea Romano, "A Design Firm Has Proposed a Cross-shaped Pool Be Built on the Rooftop of Notre Dame," Business Insider, May 30, 2019, https://www.businessinsider.com/rooftop-pool-proposal-notre-dame-cathedral-paris-photos-fire-2019-5.

166 **"the soul's longing":** "Notre Dame Reconstruction," informational document from Eight Inc.

168 **"The firefighters":** "Monseigneur Michel Aupetit: 'Le Mot Catholique N'est Pas un Gros Mot,'" Sud Radio, April 17, 2019, https://www.sudradio.fr/societe/monseigneur-michel-aupetit-le-mot-catholique-nest-pas-un-gros-mot/; Michel Aupetit, "Homélie de Mgr Michel Aupetit —Messe de la Fête de la Dédicace de la Cathédrale Notre-Dame de Paris," June 15, 2019, https://www.paris.catholique.fr/homelie-de-mgr-michel-aupetit-50850.html.

170 **"She will remain standing":** David Muir, Aicha el Hammar Castano, Esther Castillejo, and Andalmin Karamehmedovic, "Notre Dame: ABC News Gets Exclusive First Look Inside the Fire-ravaged Cathedral," ABC News, May 13, 2019, https://abcnews.go.com/International/notre-dame-abc-news-exclusive-inside-fire-ravaged/story?id=62992558.

PICTURE CREDITS

i: The New York Public Library; **ii–iii:** John Kellerman/Alamy Stock Photo; **vi–vii:** Library of Congress Prints and Photographs Division; **viii:** Library of Congress Prints and Photographs Division; **xi:** courtesy of Wikimedia Commons; **xii–1:** The New York Public Library; **2:** courtesy of Wikimedia Commons; **4:** Bibliothèque nationale de France, département Estampes et photographie, RESERVE FOL-VE-53 (G); **5:** courtesy of Wikimedia Commons; **6:** The Metropolitan Museum of Art, New York, Robert Lehman Collection, 1975; **8:** Bibliothèque nationale de France, département Estampes et photographie, RESERVE FOL-VE-53 (G); **9:** wjarek/iStock/Getty Images Plus; **10:** Terry Smith Images/Alamy Stock Photo; **12–13:** Bibliothèque Historique de la Ville de Paris (BHVP); **14:** Bibliothèque numérique de l'INHA—Provenance de l'original, Service des collections de l'Ecole Nationale Supérieure des Beaux-Arts; **15:** Library of Congress Prints and Photographs Division; **17:** Cleveland Museum of Art: French Master Drawings from the Collection of Muriel Butkin; **19:** courtesy of Rijksmuseum.nl; **20–21:** Library of Congress Prints and Photographs Division; **22:** Kirk Fisher/Alamy Stock Photo; **24:** courtesy of Wikimedia Commons/Austrian National Library; **25:** Francois Roux/Alamy Stock Photo; **26–27:** THE STORY OF BUILDINGS. Text copyright © 2014 by Patrick Dillon. Illustrations copyright © 2014 by Stephen Biesty. Reproduced by permission of the publisher, Candlewick Press, on behalf of Walker Books, London.; **28:** courtesy of Wikimedia Commons/Vassil; **29:** Godong/Alamy Stock Photo; **31:** Edwin Remsberg/Alamy Stock Photo; **32:** The Metropolitan Museum of Art, New York, David Hunter McAlpin Fund, 1944; **33:** Bibliothèque nationale de France, département Estampes et photographie, EI-13 (2643); **34–35:** Neville Mountford-Hoare/Goto-Foto/Alamy Stock Photo; **36:** Photoprofi30/iStock Editorial/Getty Images Plus; **38:** courtesy Notre-Dame de Paris © Pascal Lemaître; **39:** Kirk Fisher/Alamy Stock Photo; **40–41:** William Perry/Alamy Stock Photo; **42–43:** CDA/Guillemot/Paris, Musée Carnavalet/akg-photo; **44:** Édouard Debat-Ponsan, *Une porte du Louvre, Le matin de la Saint-Barhélemy*, 1880, huile sur toile. Clermont-Ferrand, MARQ, © Jacques-Henri Bayle; **47:** Manuel Litran/Paris Match via Getty Images; **48:** *La fete de la Raison dans Notre-Dame de Paris le 10 Novembre 1793* © Musées de Poitiers/Christian Vignaud, collection Musée de la Ville de Poitiers et de la Société des Antiquaires de l'Ouest; **50:** Hirarchivum Press/Alamy Stock Photo; **52–53:** courtesy of Wikimedia Commons/Louvre, Paris, France; **54:** Jerome Robbins Dance Division, The New York Public Library. "Frontispiece to the Esmeralda waltzes"; **55:** Internet Archive; **56:** Patrick Kovarik/AFP/Getty Images; **57:** Cleveland Museum of Art: Edwin R. and Harriet Pelton Perkins Memorial Fund;

58: Library of Congress Prints and Photographs Division; **59:** Cleveland Museum of Art: John L. Severance Fund; **60:** Library of Congress Prints and Photographs Division; **62–63:** Alfredo Garcia Saz/Alamy Stock Photo; **64:** Valery Egorov/Alamy Stock Photo; **66:** Steve Lovegrove/ Shutterstock.com; **67:** courtesy of Rijksmuseum.nl; **68–69:** Azoor Photo/Alamy Stock Photo; **70:** Artokoloro Quint Lox Limited/Alamy Stock Photo; **71:** The Miriam and Ira D. Wallach Division of Art, Prints and Photographs: Print Collection, The New York Public Library. "Le stryge."; **72:** Photopat/Alamy Stock Photo; **73:** © Marcel Fleureau / Reproduction : BHVP / Parisienne de Photographie; **74:** courtesy of Wikimedia Commons; **75:** World History Archive/ Alamy Stock Photo; **76–77:** API/Gamma-Rapho via Getty Images; **78:** Wellcome Library; **79:** Wellcome Library; **80:** Associated Press; **81:** Associated Press/Domenico Stinellis; **82:** Gaston Paris/Roger Viollet via Getty Images; **85:** Library of Congress Prints and Photographs Division; **86–87:** © Hulton-Deutsch Collection/CORBIS/Corbis via Getty Images; **88:** Galerie Bilderwelt/Getty Images; **89:** Photo 12/Alamy Stock Photo; **90:** Godong/Alamy Stock Photo; **91:** Godong/Alamy Stock Photo; **92–93:** Benny Marty/Alamy Stock Photo; **94:** Stéphanie Pourtau @blue_tinkerbell; **97:** Patrick Kovarik/AFP/Getty Images; **98–99:** Photononstop/Alamy Stock Photo; **100:** © Fonds Albert Monier, musée d'art et d'archéologie d'Aurillac; **101:** ullstein bild/ullstein bild via Getty Images; **102:** Bibliothèque nationale de France, département Estampes et photographie, EI-13 (2828); **103:** courtesy of the Library of Congress; **105:** courtesy of rijksmuseum.nl; **106:** Bruce Dale/National Geographic/Getty Images; **107:** 21567-3 : © Oswald Perrelle/Roger-Viollet; **108–9:** Keystone-France/Gamma-Rapho via Getty Images; **111:** LMPC via Getty Images; **112:** TCD/Prod.DB/Alamy Stock Photo; **113:** The Everett Collection; **114:** 6104-4: © Roger-Viollet; **115:** Karen Radkai/Condé Nast via Getty Images; **116–117:** Keystone-France/Gamma-Rapho via Getty Images; **118:** Godong/Alamy Stock Photos; **120:** courtesy Notre-Dame de Paris © Pascal Lemaître; **121:** courtesy Notre-Dame de Paris © Pascal Lemaître; **122:** The Metropolitan Museum of Art, New York, The Horace W. Goldsmith Foundation Gift, through Joyce and Robert Menschel; **123:** Bibliothèque numérique de l'INHA—Provenance de l'original Service des collections de l'Ecole Nationale Supérieure des Beaux-Arts; **125:** © ppl1958/depositphotos.com; **126:** Hemis/Alamy Stock Photo; **128:** courtesy of Wikimedia Commons/Lionel Allorge; **130:** Deliss/Godong/akg-images; **131:** Godong/Alamy Stock Photo; **132–33:** Matt Griggs/Alamy Stock Photo; **134:** Godong/Alamy Stock Photo; **135:** Godong/Alamy Stock Photo; **136–37:** Matthias Wagner/dpa picture alliance/Alamy Stock Photo; **138:** Thomas Samson/AFP/Getty Images; **141:** Veronique de Viguerie/Getty Images; **142:** Arina Lebedeva/ITAR-TASS News Agency/Alamy Stock Photo; **144–45:** Loic Salan/Shutterstock.com; **146–47:** Thomas Samson/AFP/Getty Images; **148:** Martina Badini/Shutterstock.com; **149:** Lewis Joly/Sipa via AP Images; **150:** Ludovic Marin/AFP/Getty Images; **151:** Eco Clement/UPI/Alamy Stock Photo; **153:** Godong/Alamy Stock Photo; **154:** Georges Gobet/AFP/Getty Images; **155:** Philippe Lopez/AFP/Getty Images; **157:** Christophe Petit Tesson, Pool via AP; **158:** Chesnot/Getty Images; **161:** Jacques Demarthon/AFP/Getty Images; **163:** © 2014 Ubisoft Entertainment. All Rights Reserved. Assassin's Creed, Ubisoft and the Ubisoft logo are registered or unregistered trademarks of Ubisoft Entertainment in the U.S. and/or other countries.; **164:** Ulf Mejergren Architects; **165:** © Studio NAB; **166:** POA Estudio; **167:** Eight Inc. and Tim Kobe; **168:** Karine Perret, Pool via AP; **170–71:** James L. Stanfield/National Geographic Creative.

INDEX

(*continued*)